BUSINESS ORGANISATIONS

AF510757

Legal Practice

BUSINESS ORGANISATIONS

by

Janice Shardlow

LLB, Solicitor

Senior Lecturer in Law

University of Wolverhampton

and

Peter Walton

LLB, Lecturer in Law

University of Wolverhampton

PROFESSIONAL CLP PUBLISHING

CENTRAL LAW PUBLISHING

A DIVISION OF CENTRAL LAW TRAINING LTD

© Janice Shardlow & Peter Walton 1996

Published by
CLT Professional Publishing
A Division of Central Law Training Ltd
Wrens Court
52–54 Victoria Road
Sutton Coldfield
Birmingham B72 1SX

ISBN 1 85811 089 0

All rights reserved. No part of this publication may be reproduced, stored in a retrieval system, or transmitted, in any form or by any means, electronic, mechanical, photocopying, recording or otherwise, without the prior permission of the publisher.

The moral right of the authors has been asserted.

Typeset by Adrian McLaughlin
Printed in Great Britain by Ipswich Book Ltd

Contents

Foreword

It is intended that this book will act as a handbook for those studying business law or embarking upon practice serving the needs of business clients. The approach is intentionally client-led, focusing on the key knowledge and essential skills required to deal with instructions from business clients on a continuing basis.

Janice Shardlow
Peter Walton

Table of Cases

Table of Statutes

CHAPTER 1

The Initial Choice – The Appropriate Business Medium

CHAPTER 1

The Initial Choice – The Appropriate Business Medium

The crucial choice, at least in theory, in determining the structure of a new business entity, is whether to:

- incorporate a limited company under the Companies Act 1985; *or*
- carry on the business in an unincorporated form.

It is anticipated that in most cases where a solicitor receives instructions to deal with the formalities of setting up a business, his clients will consist of more than one person. In that event, if the relationship is to be carried on in an unincorporated form, it will automatically fall within the definition of a partnership (i.e. "the carrying on of a business in common with a view of profit") and will as such be governed, to a limited extent, by the Partnership Act 1890.

In practice it is true to say that clients have often already formed a clear idea of the structure which they wish to use before they even consult a solicitor and that solicitors in the larger firms working entirely within the ambit of a corporate department may not even consider partnership as an alternative, regarding it as suitable only for the requirements of professional businesses. Nevertheless, the role of the solicitor should be to assess which structure is appropriate to the needs of the client and to advise accordingly.

In so doing the following factors should be considered:

Limited Liability

A limited company offers a clear advantage to its shareholders in that their liability, should it prove unable to pay its debts, is limited to the value of their issued shares. They are merely the owners of a separate legal person and as such are only obliged to pay the amount that they initially agreed to contribute for their ownership share. In contrast, a partnership does not constitute a separate legal person, but instead denotes the relationship between its partners, with each partner being jointly and severally liable for all partnership debts. The significance of this advantage in the current economic climate is not to be underestimated and it is often the governing factor in choosing the business medium. It is true to say that major lenders, such as banks, may well insist on personal guarantees from directors when advancing large sums to a small private company, and thus if, as is common in a small company, the directors and shareholders are in fact the same people, this advantage may be undermined to a certain extent. However the protection of limited liability will still be a crucial factor when considering other (usually trading) forms of debt.

Formality

Against the advantage of limited liability must be set the real disadvantage of the formality constraints imposed upon a limited company by the Companies Act 1985. A number of these constraints have evolved over the years with a view to protecting those who might suffer as a result of the limited liability status (e.g. rules as to maintenance of capital and publicity). However, many have been designed to deal with the separation of management from ownership which the corporate structure makes possible by placing day to day management in the hands of one body – the directors – whilst retaining ownership in another body, the shareholders.

Even where this separation of management has not in fact occurred since the directors and shareholders are the same persons, the company will nevertheless be bound to comply with the systems designed to regulate this relationship. These include detailed rules as to formal meeting procedure, the keeping of minutes and filing. To the company these formalities represent not only a constraint on its activities but also bring with them inevitable cost implications. A partnership on the other hand is subject only to the provisions of the Partnership Act 1890 (few of which represent a constraint on its operations and the majority of which can in any event be disapplied if so wished) and any voluntary constraints it chooses to impose under the terms of its partnership agreement (if any).

Publicity

The burden of formality brings with it a requirement of publicity imposed upon all companies via the filing system. Unless an unlimited company is chosen (hence losing the major advantage of limited liability referred to above) accounts will have to be filed with the Registrar of Companies together with details of directors, constitution, shareholdings etc., all of which are open to inspection by the public. There are no such requirements for partnerships.

Ability to Raise Investment

There is a widely held perception that it is easier for a company to raise money than a partnership. Certainly a company benefits from the ability to offer the security of a floating charge over all its assets to a prospective lender, thus enabling the lender, in a situation where fixed assets are inadequate, at least to obtain security over the fluctuating capital of the business. This mechanism cannot be employed to obtain security over the assets of a partnership.

It is also easier to provide a tangible investment for a new participant in a company, e.g. by means of shares or debentures, without involving him in a potential liability situation as a partner.

Cost

Due to the formality requirements imposed upon companies, the day to day running costs must inevitably exceed those of the partnership. Amongst other things the company will be required to keep minute books and file documents with Companies House, some of which, such as the annual return, must be submitted with a fee.

Ability to Extract Investment

In the case of a company, extracting the investment made may be of some difficulty particularly if made by way of shares. A company is under a duty to maintain its share capital (see p72 post) and therefore cannot return the investment to shareholders except in the strictly curtailed circumstances of a buy back of shares. It is also restricted in the amount of profit it can return to its shareholders by way of dividend. The only effective way to liquidate that investment may therefore be to transfer those shares to a new shareholder, but in the case of a small private company this may prove unrealistic and the provisions of the Companies Act 1985 and the Financial Services Act 1986 restricting the canvassing of a wide range of potential investors may effectively deter the discovery of a purchaser. Having said that, the return of an investment at the end of a debenture term is completely acceptable. A partner in contrast has a clear right to the return of his investment under the Partnership Act 1890, although of course this may be tempered by the terms of the partnership agreement itself.

Taxation

As a separate legal person, a company is subject to taxation in its own name and obliged to pay corporation tax on both income and capital profits. If it wishes to pass these profits on to its shareholders they, as separate taxable persons, will make a profit which will itself give rise to a tax liability in their hands. In simple terms this means that the corporate structure, if profits are to be fed back to shareholders, can result in a "double charge" to tax. A partnership on the other hand is not a separate legal person and its profits are attributed for tax purposes to its individual partners who are taxed accordingly by reference to the profits to which they are entitled.

Inevitably, however, there are ways, at least within a small private company, of mitigating this disadvantage and any assessment of the taxation implications of a particular structure must be considered carefully in the light of the individual circumstances of the clients involved.

Key factors

Real advantage to client of limited liability protection.
Ability/desire to operate a formal structure.
Ability/desire to bear costs.
Appropriateness of separation of management from ownership.
Desire for privacy.
Investment capacity of clients.
Investment requirements of the business.
Development plans.

Points to Watch

The client who instructs solicitors to set up a new business entity may be proposing to set up a new business from scratch. Alternatively he may be seeking to put an existing business, run either by himself as a sole trader or in conjunction with others by a *de facto* partnership, on a more formal footing. In the latter case the taking of initial instructions should involve not only an assessment of the client's future needs but also the ascertainment of the true nature of the legal structure of the business to date so that an effective transfer can be made (see p53 post).

A trading partnership cannot have more than 20 partners (s 716 Companies Act 1985). This is rarely however the decisive factor.

PART I
THE NEW CORPORATE CLIENT

CHAPTER 2

Set Up

CHAPTER 2

Set Up

Once the decision to incorporate the business has been taken, the solicitor must:

(a) Assist his clients in making a number of essential decisions as regards the formal structure of the company;

(b) Ascertain which method of effecting incorporation will best suit his clients;

(c) Obtain all requisite information from his clients; and

(d) Provide the clients with advice as to the legal implications of business activities prior to the incorporation date.

The Formal Structure

In order to set up the formal corporate structure the clients will have to make a number of vital decisions:

1. Who are the Shareholders of the Company To Be?

The answer to this question may be self-explanatory; the shareholders, and hence the owners of the company, will be the individuals who have instructed the solicitor to deal with incorporation. Sometimes, however, those individuals are incapable of raising sufficient capital to finance the activities of the company, in which case a third party, such as a venture capitalist, will also take up shares.

Technically a company is required to have at least one shareholder.

2. Who are the Officers of the Company To Be?

Directors

The directors, acting as a board will be responsible for the day to day management decisions of the company. By statute, a company must have at least one director but if Table A Articles of Association, i.e. the standard set of internal company rules referred to at p12 post is adopted, a minimum of two will be required.

Secretary

The company must have a secretary who will, *inter alia,* be responsible for the administration of the Companies Act formality requirements. If there is only one director that same person cannot also be the secretary.

3. Which Firm of Accountants is to Act as the Company's Auditors?

Every company must have an auditor whose main duty is to report to the members regarding the annual accounts. The auditor must be a qualified accountant (i.e. certified or chartered) and independent (i.e. not connected with anyone involved in the company).

4. Where is the Registered Office of the Company To Be Situated?

The company will require a registered office. This is the official address of the company and the place at which statutory books and other formal documents will be kept and documents can be served. It is important to choose an address where a careful record will be kept of communications received.

5. What is the Name of the Company To Be?

The company name is often of great importance to clients, but the choice is not as free as they might anticipate.

The choice of name will be restricted by the following rules:

(a) The name must, if the company is to be a private limited company, have the word "Limited" (or the Welsh equivalent "cyfyngedig") as its last word. This requirement can only be avoided if formal exemption is obtained under Section 30 Companies Act 1985. In addition the word "Limited" (or cyfyngedig) must not appear elsewhere in the name either in full or in an abbreviated form.

(b) The name must not be the same as one which already appears in the Registrar of Companies' Index of Company Names.

(c) It must not be a name the use of which, in the opinion of the Secretary of State, constitutes a criminal offence.

(d) It must not be a name which, in the opinion of the Secretary of State, is offensive.

(e) If in the opinion of the Secretary of State the name would be likely to give the impression that the company is connected in any way with Her Majesty's government or with any local authority, then the Secretary of State's approval for its use must be given.

(f) If it includes any word or expression contained in the Company and Business Names Regulations 1981, then approval must be obtained from the body designated in those regulations.

(g) If the name is already registered as a trademark, then its use will constitute a breach of that trademark.

(h) If the name misleads third parties to assume that the company is in fact a similarly named business, a passing off action may result.

(i) If, once the name is registered, the Secretary of State is of the opinion that the name gives so misleading an indication of the nature of its activities as to be likely to cause harm to the public, he can direct that the name should be changed.

CHECKLIST: NAME

1. Ask the clients for a list of acceptable names.
2. Discount any names which run the risk of being considered offensive, use of which may be a criminal offence or use of which may be considered to be so misleading as to cause harm to the public. Consider carefully if any word which suggests a link with Her Majesty's Government of a local authority is likely to obtain approval and advise the clients accordingly.
3. In view of the inability to reserve a name and therefore the possibility that after inspecting the Index of Company Names but before filing another company may take the desired name, advise the clients not to expend money on stationery until a Certificate of Incorporation bearing an appropriate name has been obtained.
4. Advise the clients re passing off and either check trade directories personally or ensure that the clients do this. Consider direct communication with any potential claimants.

5. Check the chosen names against the Index of Company Names. Discount those where an identical name is registered, consider carefully the risk of passing off where a similar name appears. If necessary communicate direct with the current user.
6. Check the Company and Business Names Regulations 1981 and if necessary prepare a letter requesting approval.
7. Check Trademarks Register if appropriate.
8. If a substantial delay has occurred since the initial check of the Index, carry out a further check before submission of the documents.

6. What are the Formal Objects of the Company as Stated in the Memorandum of Association of the Company To Be?

The memorandum of association is one of the two constitutional documents of the company, and is designed to deal with the company's external relationships. It must, *inter alia,* contain a formal statement of the objects of the company, i.e. set out the parameters of the operations of this artificial legal entity. In the past this statement has caused innumerable problems due to the doctrine of *ultra vires*, the principle that as an artificial legal person a company could not validly exceed its stated parameters of operation. As a result over the years this part of the memorandum became increasingly lengthy as draftsmen sought to ensure that the company they were forming would not fall foul of this doctrine.

The principle of *ultra vires* has however now been tempered by a number of legislative provisions:

Section 3A Companies Act 1985

This provides quite simply that if the memorandum of a company states that its object is "to carry on business as a general commercial company", then the object of that company is to carry on any trade or business whatsoever and it has power to do all things incidental or conducive to the carrying on of any trade or business by it. An example of a memorandum using this format is set out at p17 post.

Section 35 Companies Act 1985

This provides that the validity of an act done by a company cannot be called into question by reason of anything in the company's memorandum. However, it also provides that the members have a power to restrain the doing of an act which but for this provision would be beyond the company's capacity and the directors are still bound by the duty to observe the limitations in the memorandum. Any act in breach of this duty can only be ratified by a special resolution.

Section 35A Companies Act 1985

This provides that in favour of a person dealing with the company in good faith, the power of the directors to bind the company, or authorise others to do so, is deemed to be free of any limitation under the company's constitution. However it also provides, *inter alia,* that this does not affect any right of a member of the company to bring proceedings to restrain the doing of an act which is beyond the powers of the directors.

The implications would appear to be:

1. If the general commercial company format is adopted the risk of *ultra vires* is greatly diminished since the company can carry out any trade or business and anything reasonably incidental or conducive to any of those trades or businesses.
2. Even if the general commercial format is not adopted, any *ultra vires* act will not be invalid and the company will still be able to rely on it as a valid act. However the members may, if they become aware of the proposal, prevent it being carried out and the directors will still bear liability for it unless their acts are ratified.

Clients should accordingly be advised to adopt the general commercial company format which will result in a simple and straightforward form of memorandum as envisaged by the legislators.

Points to Watch
Advisors should however take note of the following:

It has been observed that the provisions of Section 3A as to incidental activities rely on an objective assessment of the incidental and conducive nature. In some quarters it is therefore thought appropriate to add to the simplicity of the general commercial object a traditional object in the form similar to that used in the case of *Bell Houses Ltd* v *City Wall Properties Ltd* [1966] 1 QB 207 (hence its designation as a "Bell Houses clause") which extends the ambit to those activities thought by the directors to be conducive etc.

Example of a Bell Houses clause

"to carry on any other trade or business whatsoever which can, in the opinion of the board of directors, be advantageously carried on by the company in connection with or ancillary to any of the above business or the general business of the company."

The use of this provision may itself necessitate the use of a *"Cotman* v *Brougham"* clause (see below).

Clients often appear to prefer an actual statement of their envisaged aims for the company and may feel that such a statement may be more acceptable to potential creditors. Any attempt to include this within the general commercial company format runs the risk of invoking the main objects clause doctrine.

This doctrine provides that the first object of a memorandum is the main one and all the other objects must be read as subsidiary to that first object. It is therefore necessary to set out a clause in a form similar to that used in the case of *Cotman* v *Brougham* [1918] AC 518 (hence known as a "*Cotman* v *Brougham* clause") which will effectively displace this doctrine and allow all clauses to be treated as being of equal weight.

Example of a *Cotman* v *Brougham* clause.

"Every sub-clause is to be construed as a substantive clause and is not to be limited or restricted by references to any other sub-clause or by the name of the company, and no sub-clause nor the objects specified therein is to be deemed subsidiary or auxiliary merely to the objects mentioned in the first sub-clause".

7. What is the Share Capital of the Company To Be?

This effectively involves consideration of two issues:

1. What is the *Authorised* Share Capital of the Company To Be?
The memorandum of association must contain a clause which sets out the share capital which the company is authorised to issue (see p17 post). The figure stated is not necessarily the actual share capital which it is envisaged will be issued: it is rather a ceiling figure, i.e. capital cannot be issued in excess of this figure without making a change to this part of the memorandum. Since no further expense is entailed in inserting a high figure, but any change

should the figure prove inadequate will result in the expense of holding a general meeting, it is suggested that the initial figure should be reasonably high.

2. What is the *Issued* Share Capital of the Company To Be?
This term is used to refer to the amount of capital which is actually issued. The level will, of necessity, depend on the financial requirements of the business and the capacity of the shareholders.

Clients should be advised that tax relief, by way of deduction of interest paid as a charge on income, is available where a loan is obtained to enable the borrower to acquire shares in a close trading company (many small companies will fall within this definition – see p42 post). To be eligible it is necessary that at the time the interest is paid the individual concerned either:

(a) has a material interest in the company i.e. control of more than 5% of the ordinary share capital; or
(b) is a shareholder and works for the greater part of his time, i.e. 50% in the actual management or conduct of the business.

Point to Watch
Shares cannot be issued at a discount, i.e. for a consideration less than their nominal value. It is however possible for the consideration to be paid in part only (leading to "partly-paid shares"), until "a call" is made for the balance of the sum outstanding. The amount paid up at any one time is known as "paid-up" share capital.

8. Is it Acceptable to use the Standard Table A Format as the Articles of Association of the Company or are Alternative Provisions Required?

The articles of association is the second constitutional document of the company, its role being to set out the rules which will govern the internal conduct of the company. A set of such rules designed to cater for the needs of the average private company is provided in what is known as "Table A", currently contained in the Companies (Tables A to F) Regulations 1985 SI 1985/805.

A company can either:
(a) adopt this set of rules;
(b) prepare its own completely separate "special" set of articles; or
(c) adopt Table A as modified by a number of its own special articles designed to deal with the areas where Table A is inappropriate for its needs.

An assessment must therefore be made in each case of the suitability of Table A to the clients needs. The current Table A is arguably unsuitable for most companies in that it does not provide a Section 80 authority without which no shares can be issued without first holding a general meeting and passing a resolution to confer this authority. It is therefore suggested that at the very least a special Article should be adopted to this effect.

In addition it is suggested that the following questions should be asked:
(a) Is it intended that ownership of the company should remain in the hands of the people initially designated as shareholders?
If so special Articles should be drafted to:
(i) Widen the powers of the directors to refuse to register transfers of shares;
(ii) Restrict the rights of shareholders to make such transfers;
(iii) Tighten the provisions of Section 89 Companies Act 1985 on the issue of new shares.

(b) Is it intended that those appointed as directors should be appointed on a permanent basis?
If so:
  (i) Articles 73–75 of Table A (retirement by rotation) should be excluded;
  (ii) A clause to increase a director's voting rights on a resolution to remove him from office (a "*Bushell* v *Faith* clause") should be inserted (see p67 post).

(c) Are the same persons to be both directors and shareholders?
If so:
  (i) Consider the exclusion of Articles 94–95 which prevent a director from voting on an issue in which he has an interest;
  (ii) Consider the appropriateness of the Table A quorum requirements.

9. Is a Shareholders' Agreement Required?

As a public document the Articles of Association may not be an appropriate place to set out matters which the shareholders have agreed but wish to keep private. In addition, although the Articles act as a contract between the company and members and between the members themselves; they are always open to alteration by special resolution. It should also be noted that shareholders can only enforce rights under the Articles given to them in their capacity as shareholders and not in any outsider capacity, e.g. director, promoter, solicitor, vendor of property. If the shareholders wish to enter into contractual obligations between themselves of an enduring enforceable nature it is therefore necessary to enter into a separate contract. These contracts are commonly known as shareholders' agreements.

10. What is the Company's Accounting Reference Date To Be?

The company is obliged to make up accounts on an annual basis. If it fails to notify the Registrar of Companies of its preferred date for making up its accounts within nine months of incorporation it will have to make up accounts to the date of the last day of the month in which the anniversary of its incorporation date falls.

11. Do the Clients Wish to Use a Company Seal?

It is no longer necessary for a company to use a company seal. Some clients do however still prefer to use one, and their wishes in this area must be ascertained so that the correct seal can be ordered.

12. Do the Clients Feel it is Appropriate to Adopt the Elective Regime?

The term "elective regime" refers to the ability of the members of a company to relax the following five Companies Act requirements which may be thought by the members of small private companies to be unnecessarily stringent:

	Requirement		Form of relaxation
1.	That a company must hold an Annual General Meeting (AGM) each year.	1.	No AGM required to be held, unless requested by a member.
2.	That the accounts and reports of a company must be laid before a general meeting of its members each year.	2.	Accounts must still be prepared, but need not be put before members at an AGM.
3.	That the auditors of a company must be appointed annually.	3.	Indefinite appointment possible.
4.	That directors can only be authorised to issue shares for a maximum of 5 years' period.	4.	Members can specify that the authority is to last for a fixed period of time in excess of 5 years or even indefinitely.
5.	That Extraordinary General Meetings (EGM) can only be called on short notice if a majority of members holding at least 95% of shares agree to do so.	5.	Figure can be reduced to a minimum of 90%.

In particular where the directors and shareholders are largely the same persons, it may be felt that all or some of these relaxations may be beneficial. In that case it will be necessary for the members of the company to pass elective resolutions at an early stage to make the necessary changes (see p35 post). This will require, *inter alia,* unanimity.

INITIAL INSTRUCTIONS CHECKLIST

1. Shareholders
2. Directors
3. Secretary
4. Auditors
5. Registered office
6. Name
7. Objects
8. Share capital
9. Articles
10. Shareholders' agreement
11. Accounting reference date
12. Seal
13. Elective regime

Creating a Company

1. "Tailor Made" Companies

The solicitor can incorporate the company from scratch for his clients, "tailor making" the company so that it meets their precise needs. Such an operation inevitably takes time, not necessarily in the drafting of the Memorandum and Articles of Association, which can be effected relatively quickly using modern technology, but in the delay between drafting and obtaining signatures to the relevant documentation, dispatching those to Companies House and awaiting the certificate of incorporation.

Even this process can however now be short-circuited at Companies House by paying an increased fee, currently £200, and using the Companies House Fast Track incorporation service. Provided that documents are submitted to Companies House or one of its branches before 3 p.m. on the day in question, all documents are in order and the company name does not require approval, incorporation can be effected on that day.

Shelf Companies

The solicitor may on the other hand feel that it is more appropriate to use a shelf company. This is a company which has already been incorporated and is literally sitting "on a shelf" awaiting use. Depending on the size of its corporate practice, a firm of solicitors may have set up a series of these shelf companies in anticipation of the needs of its clients. Since such a company has already been incorporated it can be transferred to the clients immediately, allowing business activities to commence without delay. The company will have been set up in a form which the solicitor believes is most suitable to the needs of his clients, and so any alterations (other than to name, registered office and personnel) should be minimal.

Should a solicitors' firm not have such a company available, it is possible to purchase such a shelf company from a company formation agent and to benefit from the company being already incorporated and ready for use. In these circumstances however the company may require more substantial alterations if it is to meet the requirements of the clients, which will inevitably increase costs. Some care will be required to ensure that the transfer of the company is properly carried out, since the format provided is by no means of a uniform nature.

Key factors
Timing
Cost
Memorandum: general commercial company
Articles: suitability

Essential Information

The following information will be required whether incorporation is from scratch or a shelf company is utilised:

Name
- first choice;
- acceptable alternatives.

Registered office
- address.

Proposed company activity

Details of directors:
- full name;
- any previous names (other than maiden names);
- date of birth;
- nationality;
- business occupation;
- residential address;
- other directorships.

Details of Secretary:
- full name;
- any previous names (other than maiden name);
- residential address.

> **Point to Watch**
> Although the obtaining of this information would appear to be a somewhat tedious process, it is essential to keep to a checklist and to request all requisite information in one go. Nothing looks worse than having to return to the clients because one or more trivial but essential pieces of information are missing or even subsequently having to return to Companies House to effect an amendment.

> ***Practical Tip***
> **If using existing client information e.g. copy company search containing directors details, submit a copy to the clients with a request for confirmation that this is up to date.**

Business Activities Prior to the Incorporation Date

Clients are, not surprisingly, keen to get on with running their new business and often perceive the legal technicalities of incorporation as something to be organised by the solicitor whilst they proceed with this important task. Conscious of this, the solicitor must:

(a) Advise the clients as to the likely time delay, depending, of course, on the method of incorporation;

(b) Emphasise what, to the solicitor, may be the obvious point, that a company does not exist as a legal person until a certificate of incorporation is issued, and ensure that specific advice on pre-incorporation contracts is given to the clients, preferably in writing. The position is relatively simple; Section 36C Companies Act 1985 makes it clear that if a person purports to act for the company or as agent for it and a contract is entered into or a deed executed which purports to be made by or on behalf of a company at a time when the company has not been formed, then that person will, subject to any agreement to the contrary, be personally liable on the contract. Contracts purportedly made by the company before the date of its incorporation will therefore render the individuals involved personally liable unless the third party, which is unlikely, agrees otherwise. The safest course must therefore be to await incorporation before entering into contracts. If this is not acceptable to the clients it may be that the wrong method of incorporation has been chosen due to an incorrect assessment of the speed element.

Incorporation

The solicitor will need to prepare and submit the following to the Registrar of Companies together with the incorporation fee, currently £20:

1. Form 10: statement of first directors and secretary and intended situation of registered office.
2. Form G12: statutory declaration of compliance with requirements on application for registration of a company.
3. Memorandum of Association
4. Articles of Association

> **Point to Watch**
> Any letter requesting approval of the use of a name should be sent with the incorporation documents.

Documents and Forms

1. Form 10

Ensure that all directors and secretary sign the consent to act and that all their details are complete.

2. Form G12

Note that although there is a box for the company number this is not yet known and cannot be inserted. If the declaration is to be sworn by the acting solicitor, it must not be sworn before a solicitor in the same firm.

3. Memorandum of Association

THE COMPANIES ACT 1985

PRIVATE COMPANY LIMITED BY SHARES

MEMORANDUM OF ASSOCIATION OF "   Limited"

1. The Company's name is ________________________[1].
2. The Company's registered office is to be situated in England and Wales[2].
3. The object of the company is to carry on business as a general commercial company.[3].
4. The liability of the Members is limited[4].
5. The Company's share capital is divided into _____ shares of _____ each[5].

WE, the subscribers to this Memorandum of Association, wish to be formed into a Company pursuant to this Memorandum; and we agree to take the number of shares shown opposite our respective names[6].	
Names and addresses of Subscribers	Number of shares taken by each Subscriber
	Total shares taken
Dated this Witness to the above Signatures:	

Notes

[1] Name clause: see p9 ante

[2] Office clause: this must state the country in which the registered office will be found (NB this is the one clause of the Memorandum that cannot be altered once incorporation has occurred)

[3] Objects: see p10 ante

[4] Liability: in the case of a limited liability company this will simply be a statement to that effect.

[5] Capital: see p11 ante.

[6] Association and subscription clause: this is a formal statement to the effect that the subscribers (of whom there must be at least one) declare their wish to be formed into a company under the memorandum; and agree to take at least one share in the company.
Note: these subscribers will become the first members of the company on incorporation. They are the only people who can ever be members of the company without having had shares issued to them. Each subscriber must state name, address and occupation, and must sign the Memorandum in the presence of a witness. The Memorandum will then be dated.

4. *Articles of Association*

These must be:

(a) printed;
(b) divided into paragraphs numbered consecutively;
(c) signed by each subscriber to the Memorandum in the presence of at least one witness who must attest the signatures.

If, as is common, Table A is to be adopted in part only, the Articles will commence with a provision in similar form to the following:

> *"The Regulations contained or incorporated in Table A as prescribed by the Companies (Tables A to F) Regulations SI 1985/805 other than Regulations shall apply to the Company and together with the regulations which follow, shall constitute the Articles of Association of the Company".*

TABLE A: ARTICLES ALTERATIONS CHECKLIST

1. Insert Section 80 Companies Act 1985 authority.
2. Article 24 – widen powers of directors to refuse to register transfers of shares.
3. Insert pre-emption rights on transfer.
4. Either relax Section 89 Companies Act 1985 provisions or tighten them up as appropriate.
5. Remove retirement by rotation Articles 73–75.
6. Insert *Bushell* v *Faith* clause.
7. Alter quorum requirements, Articles 40 and 89.
8. Remove chairman's casting vote.
9. Remove Articles 94–95.
10. Extend lien in Article 8 to fully paid shares and all indebtedness.
11. Insert maximum/minimum number of directors.
12. Insert provision to force election on transmission of shares on receipt of notice, amending Article 30.
13. Relax poll demand requirements, amending Article 46.
14. Insert additional provisions to enable a director to be removed without prejudice to Sections 303, 304 Companies Act 1985.
15. Insert provision for directors' meetings by means of telephone, video conferencing etc.
16. Insert express power to borrow.

Post-incorporation

On receipt of the certificate of incorporation the clients should be notified immediately of the incorporation date. The solicitor should then:

1. Hold the first board meeting;
2. Deal with all external filing requirements;
3. Complete the statutory books; *and*
4. Despatch the completed books to the client.

First Board Meeting

The aim of the first board meeting is to put the company into a position where it can commence trading forthwith. If the company has been incorporated by solicitors it is usual to prepare the board minutes on the client's behalf, assist the directors in conducting the meeting and then, having written up the company books and filed the requisite documents, deliver the completed books to the company.

The precise contents of the board minutes may vary, but the following comprises a checklist of a standard agenda:

FIRST BOARD MEETING CHECKLIST

1. Report incorporation.
2. Report appointment of directors and secretary.
3. Appoint chairman.
4. Adopt seal (optional).
5. Appoint auditors.
6. Determine accounting reference date.
7. Appoint bankers and deal with bank mandate.
8. Arrange VAT registration if appropriate.
9. Receive applications for shares and Section 317 declarations if appropriate.
10. Allot shares (including subscriber shares).
11. Receive notifications of Section 324 interests.
12. Receive general notifications of Section 317 interests.
13. Approve payment of costs of formation.

FILING REQUIREMENTS CHECKLIST

To the Registrar of Companies
Form 224: notification of accounting reference date.
Form 88(2): allotment of shares for cash

Internal Filing
Minutes
Register of Directors
Register of Company Secretaries
Register of Members
Register of Directors' Interests

Points to Watch

i) The subscriber shares are not issued on incorporation. They must therefore be formally issued, although they are not applied for, since the subscribers have already agreed to take them.

ii) Although a general declaration of directors' interests in other businesses is usually made (see p29 post), there is no register of Section 317 interests.

iii) If the company will be making taxable supplies, it should apply for voluntary VAT registration if the set-off of VAT it pays on supplies received against supplies it makes will work to its advantage. Registration becomes compulsory where either taxable supplies in the last 12 months exceeds £47,000 or if there are reasonable grounds for believing that the value of taxable supplies in the ensuing 30 days will mean that the figure is exceeded.

iv) A Section 324 Companies Act 1985 declaration must be made when a director or a member of his close family becomes interested in the shares or debentures of the company. A register is kept of these declarations, the Register of Directors' Interests.

Practical Tip

The Register of Members should first be completed on incorporation when the subscribers are entered as members but not shareholders.

Copies of all forms registered with the Registrar of Companies should be kept at the back of the statutory books. This enables a simple check on filing compliance to be made.

Shelf Company Format

The form in which shelf companies are delivered varies and great care must be taken to deal with the documentation supplied correctly. It will always be necessary to change directors, secretary, registered office and shareholders, however further changes, of a more complex procedural nature will be required if the answer to any of the following questions is in the negative.

- Is the Memorandum suitable?
- Are the Articles suitable?
- Is the existing name or the use of a business name acceptable?
- Is the capital clause sufficient?

CHECKLIST OF CHANGES WHICH MAY BE REQUIRED

		Filing Requirements		
Change	*Method of Change*	*Internal*	*To Registrar of Companies*	*Notes*
Directors	Board resolution	Register of Directors (Register of Directors' Interests if s 324 declaration made), Board minutes	Form 288a Form 288b	Consider whether s 324 declaration and general s 317 declaration appropriate
Secretary	Board resolution	Register of Secretaries, Board minutes	Form 288a Form 288b	
Registered Office	Board resolution	Board minutes	Form 287	
Share transfer	Transferor completes stock transfer form and hands with share certificate to transferee. Transferee presents properly stamped transfer to company	Register of Members		The company is obliged to enter the transferee's name in the Register of Members within 2 months unless a positive decision to refuse to register is made
Name	Special resolution	Board minutes, minutes of General Meeting	Print of resolution. £20. Print of new memorandum	(i) formal letter requesting approval of name may be required, see p9. (ii) name cannot be used until Certificate of Incorporation on change of name is issued
Objects	Special resolution	Board minutes, minutes of General Meeting	Print of resolut-ion. Print of new memorandum	See p56
Authorised share capital	Ordinary resolution	Board minutes, minutes of General Meeting	Print of resolution. Form 123. Print of new memorandum	This is one of the exceptional ordinary resolutions which must be filed
Articles	Special resolution	Board minutes, minutes of General Meeting	Print of resolution. New Articles	

Any board resolutions must be passed by simple majority at a duly convened meeting of the directors or by unanimous written resolution (see p28 post). Where an ordinary or special resolution is required this refers to a resolution of the members passed at a duly convened general meeting by the requisite majority. In the case of an ordinary resolution this is over 50% and in the case of a special resolution at least 75%.

Normally a fixed length of notice to members is required before a general meeting of the members can be held (14 clear days where an ordinary resolution is to be considered and 21 clear days where the resolution is a special resolution). It is however possible to have a lesser period of notice if a "consent to short notice" is completed. In the case of an Extraordinary General Meeting, this requires the consent of a majority in number of members holding not less than 95% in nominal value of shares giving a right to attend and vote at the general meeting.

CONSENT TO SHORT NOTICE

[ ] LIMITED ("the Company")

We, the undersigned, being together a majority in number of the members of the Company together holding not less than 95% in nominal value of the shares giving the right to attend and vote at the Extraordinary General Meeting covened by the attached notice HEREBY CONSENT to the holding of that meeting and to the proposing and passing at that meeting as Special [and Ordinary] Resolutions of the Resolutions set out in the attached notice notwithstanding that shorter notice than that specified in the Companies Act 1985 and in the Company's Articles of Association has been given.

Dated 199

....

This effectively means that, subject to the obtaining of such consent, it is possible to hold the general meeting a matter of minutes after the board meeting and the whole procedure can therefore be dealt with in a short period of time. We will refer to this method of proceeding throughout this book as the "quick meeting procedure".

THE QUICK MEETING PROCEDURE CHECKLIST

Board meeting (called on reasonable notice)

1. Report on proposal.
2. Resolve to convene general meeting on short notice to pass necessary resolution.
3. Adjourn board meeting.

General Meeting (held after obtaining signatures to consent to short notice)

1. Agree that agenda is taken as read.
2. Pass resolution.
3. Close meeting.

Board meeting

4. Formally reconvene board meeting.
5. Report on passing of requisite resolution.
6. Effect any consequential matters.
7. Instruct secretary to deal with formalities.
8. Close meeting.

Points to Watch

A written notice of the general meeting conforming with the requirements set out at p33 post will still be required.

If the directors and shareholders are the same persons, the solicitor must take care to ensure that at any point in time they are aware of the capacity in which they are acting.

EXAMPLE: CONTENTS OF A TYPICAL SHELF COMPANY PACK

1. Certificate of incorporation
2. Memorandum of association (general commercial company)
3. Articles of Association (Table A with Article 80 authority)
4. Minutes of First Board meeting showing:
   change of registered office
   appointment of new directors
   appointment of new secretary
   resignation of existing directors/secretary after close of meeting
5. Undated stock transfer forms

PROCEDURE REQUIRED TO TRANSFER TYPICAL SHELF COMPANY TO CLIENTS

Second Board Meeting

1. Report on first board meeting – registered office, directors, secretary etc.
2. Appointment of chairman.
3. Instruction to secretary to register subscribers as members.
4. Issue of subscriber shares and receipt of consideration for them.
5. Receipt of stock transfer forms re subscriber shares duly stamped.
6. Approval of transfers and instruction to secretary to register transferees as members and to issue share certificates in due course.
7. Report that GM required to:
   - alter name
   - alter authorised share capital
   - alter Articles
8. Resolution to call EGM and instruction to secretary to deal with notices and consent to short notice.
9. Adjourn board meeting.

General Meeting

1. Agree that agenda is taken as read.
2. Vote on resolutions:
   - name – special resolution;
   - share capital – ordinary resolution;
   - articles – special resolution
3. Close meeting.

Board meeting

10. Reconvene board meeting.
11. Report on GM.
12. Instruct Secretary to file :
    - print of resolutions;
    - Form 123;
    - amended memorandum;
    - awarded Articles;
    - fee of £20 re change of name.
13. Receive Section 317 general declarations.
14. Receive Section 324 declarations and instruct secretary to complete Register of Directors' Interests.
15. Deal with all matters normally dealt with at first board meeting.
16. Close meeting.

Points to Watch

It is possible that the pack will not actually provide for the shares to be transferred but will instead contain renounceable letters of allotment and the subscribers renounce their rights to the shares they have agreed to take in favour of the solicitor's clients. This method became common in the 1970s when it was used as part of a scheme to avoid capital duty. Capital duty has been abolished and there is no initial stamp duty advantage in using this method. It may well however still be used as part of more detailed stamp duty planning if a reorganisation is occurring.

CHAPTER 3

Day to Day Running

CHAPTER 3

Day to Day Running

Ideally, the solicitor's involvement will not end with the despatch of the certificate of incorporation and statutory books to the clients. Instead he will then become involved in advising the new client – the company – on its day to day running .

The Articles of the company will play a central role when giving this advice. Most companies will have adopted a set of articles incorporating a substantial part of Table A, and therefore the following discussion deals predominantly with those provisions and the standard amendments which may have been adopted.

Points to Watch

It should not be forgotten that apart from the small number of provisions which must be followed since they are dictated by statute, the content of the Articles can, at least in theory, vary considerably. There is no substitute for looking at the particular Articles of the company concerned.

In 1984/5 alone three versions of Table A were in fact published. A company which adopted Table A Articles in whole or in part during this period may therefore have adopted any one of three versions. It is clearly essential to identify the correct version. This task will be made easier if a copy of the Table A in force at the date of incorporation has, as is good practice, been kept with the company books.

Directors

The new directors of the company, from whom the solicitor will receive instructions on behalf of the company, will, quite rightly, on incorporation assume the role of running the company on a day to day basis. Their technical authority to do so will be contained in the Articles of the company usually in a form similar to that contained in Table A. Article 70 Table A provides that the business of the company shall be managed by the directors and that subject to the Act, the Memorandum and Articles and any direction given by the members by special resolution, they may exercise all the powers of the company.

A person who takes on the position of director of a company must however be aware that he is taking on a position of trust, in essence the managing of a separate legal entity which, since it is not an actual person, cannot manage itself. A director places himself in a fiduciary position, and therefore cannot simply behave as he wishes out of motives of self interest, but must act in the best interests of the company in accordance with a number of principles, known as fiduciary duties.

These duties are owed to the company itself, not to the individuals who have invested in the company, and therefore if they are breached it is (as a general rule) the company which must seek redress by requiring the director concerned to compensate the company for any loss suffered and/or to account to the company for any profit made.

Traditionally this fiduciary position is treated as being subject to three particular aspects:

1. Duty Not to Make a Secret Profit

Obviously a director is in a privileged position as regards the company and may often find that the information/contacts gained in that position could be used for personal profit. However, if they are used in that way, he will be obliged to account to the company for any profit made unless:

(a) all relevant facts are fully disclosed to the members of the company and their approval (known as ratification) is obtained by ordinary resolution; *or*
(b) if the company's Articles incorporate Article 85 Table A, he fully discloses the nature and extent of any material interest to the other directors.

2. Duty Not to Exceed or Abuse Powers

A director is not only under a duty not to exceed his powers, but must also ensure that he does not abuse them by using them for the wrong motives. This is of particular relevance when one looks at the power to issue shares. This power must only be exercised for the purpose for which it was given to the directors – to raise capital for the company – and not, for instance, to ensure that certain shareholders have sufficient shares to outvote others.

If a director abuses his powers, again it is possible in certain circumstances for the members in general meeting to ratify the breach by ordinary resolution.

3. Duty to Act with Skill and Care

The director has a duty to act with skill and care. Until recently it was assumed that this duty was not particularly stringent. Recent case law has clarified the area, likening this common law duty to the statutory liability for wrongful trading of a director of an insolvent company. The standard of care expected is that of a reasonably diligent person having both:

(a) the general knowledge, skill and experience that may reasonably be expected of a person carrying out the same functions as are carried out by that director in relation to the company; and
(b) the general knowledge, skill and experience that the director has.

There is therefore an objective minimum standard of competence expected. If the director has some special skill or knowledge he will be judged subjectively at that higher level. Once again, breaches of this duty are capable of ratification by the members passing an ordinary resolution.

Points to Watch
As has been noted, some breaches of duty are capable of ratification by the members. This has the effect of wiping the slate clean and preventing the company subsequently bringing misfeasance proceedings against the director. It should be noted that not all breaches of duty are capable of ratification. Some breaches are regarded as a "fraud on the minority" and therefore outside the power of the members to ratify. In such circumstances the director's potential liability for breach of duty remains open.

Directors' Meetings

The powers given to the directors are given to them as a collective body, the board of directors. These powers must therefore be exercised by the board, unless the board has itself appointed a single director or a committee of directors as its delegate to operate a particular power (Art 72 Table A).

It is relatively common for the directors to appoint a managing director and to delegate some of its powers to such a person. The office of managing director will however automatically terminate if that person ceases to be a director.

The board makes its decisions as to the exercise of its powers by passing resolutions. The traditional way to pass resolutions is to hold a meeting of the board, but it is also possible to pass such resolutions by written resolution (see specimen form) without holding such a meeting. However, in this case unanimity is required if the resolution is to be passed (Art 93 Table A).

WRITTEN RESOLUTIONS OF DIRECTORS

[ ] LIMITED

Registered Number:

Incorporated on 199

Made pursuant to Regulation 93 of Table A in the Companies (Tables A to F) Regulations 1985.

IT IS HEREBY RESOLVED as follows:

1. that [ ].

2. that [ ].

Dated .... 199[ ]

Signed ....

Signed ....

Signed ....

A board meeting may be called either by a director or the secretary at the request of a director by giving notice to all the directors (including alternate directors) other than a director who is absent from the UK. There is no fixed time limit for this notice, however it must be reasonable.

In order for the board meeting to pass valid resolutions the meeting must be quorate. Table A provides that the quorum is two.

Resolutions are passed by a simple majority. If such a majority is not achieved the resolution fails and the status quo remains. Table A provides for the chairman to have a casting vote in the case of equality, but this provision is rightly often excluded where there is an even number of directors.

Passing a Resolution with an Even Number of Directors, One of whom is Chairman with a Casting Vote.

Example 1
Four directors vote, A, B, C, & D. A is chairman.
A & B in favour, C & D against. A uses casting vote to win.
C & D in favour, A & B against. Resolution fails, status quo remains.

Example 2
Two directors vote, E & F. E is chairman.
E is in favour, F against. E uses casting vote to win.
F is in favour, E against. Resolution fails, status quo remains.

A director who wishes to ensure that he is represented at a meeting even though he cannot always attend can appoint an "alternate director" (Arts 65–69 Table A) by giving notice to the company. This alternate director will be entitled to notices of all meetings and to attend and vote at those meetings when his appointor cannot attend.

Point to Watch
There is some debate as to whether the appointment of an alternate should be notified to the Registrar of Companies on Form 288a and whether his name should be entered in the Register of Directors.

Resolutions Subject to Further Procedural Constraints where a Director may have a Conflict of Interest

(a) Entering into Contracts in which a Director is Interested

A director interested in any way, directly or indirectly, in a contract or proposed contract with the company, is obliged under Section 317 Companies Act 1985 to declare the nature of that interest at a meeting of the directors of the company (see specimen form P30). Any director failing to do so is liable to a fine. The term contract includes any transaction or arrangement and any loan or quasi loan covered by Section 330 Companies Act 1985 (see p32 post).

Notice should be either specific or general. A specific notice should state that the director is interested in a particular contract and be given at the first meeting when the contract is discussed or the first meeting when the director becomes interested in the contract, whichever is the earlier. Alternatively, it is possible to give what is known as a general notice to the effect that the director is a member of a named company or firm, or connected with a named person, and is to be regarded thereafter as interested in any contract which may be made with that company, firm or person. Such general notice enables the interested director to avoid the risk of overlooking the disclosure at a later stage: the corollary is that his fellow directors may, to his advantage, overlook the fact that an interest has been disclosed when considering the contract.

It should be noted that since there is no register of Section 317 interests the only way to check up on prior notices is to go back through the minutes of the company.

GENERAL SECTION 317 NOTICE

To: The Secretary,
[ ] Limited,
[Address]

Pursuant to sub-section 317(3) of the Companies Act 1985 **I GIVE YOU NOTICE** that I have an interest in the following companies and firms and that I am to be regarded as interested in any contract which might be made with such company or firm:

Company or Firm	**Nature of Interest**

Dated 199

....
(Director)

(b) Matters in Which the Director is Interested

In addition to the statutory requirements of disclosure of interests in contracts, Table A provides that a director may not vote (Art 94 Table A) or count in the quorum (Art 95 Table A) at a meeting on any resolution concerning a matter in which he, or a person connected with him (or if an alternate, his appointor) has, directly or indirectly, an interest or duty which is material and which conflicts or may conflict with the interests of the company. This obligation is however subject to four exceptions including, *inter alia,* an interest which arises by virtue of his subscription for shares in the company. If there is any doubt as to the application of Article 94 Table A at a meeting, the Chairman's ruling is conclusive.

Although Article 96 Table A provides that these provisions can be suspended or relaxed by ordinary resolution it may well have been felt when incorporating the company that the protection of Section 317 was sufficient and that such Articles were not included in the Articles of Association of the company. This is obviously particularly important when there are only two directors.

(c) Directors' Service Contracts

Directors appointed solely to that office and not to an executive position in the company (and therefore often referred to as non-executives) will not require a service contract. They will only be entitled to remuneration as determined by the company by ordinary resolution (Art 82 Table A) and to expenses properly incurred in connection with their attendance at meetings or otherwise in connection with the discharge of their duties. The vast majority of directors will however perform other duties of an executive nature and their appointment to this executive position can be made upon such terms as the directors themselves determine and for such remuneration as they think fit.

Since the director will clearly be interested in his own service contract, he must declare this interest to the board in compliance with Section 317. His interest will also fall within the ambit of Article 94 Table A and therefore will disallow him from voting or counting in the quorum. Obviously this is yet one more reason for disapplying Article 94 Table A *et seq.*, particularly in a two-director company where this provision will effectively prevent approval of a directors' contract without shareholder approval via a relaxation of Article 94 Table A.

If the contract is for a fixed term exceeding five years prior consent must in any event be obtained from members in general meeting by ordinary resolution under Section 319 Companies Act 1985. All terms of the service contract must be available for inspection by the members at the registered office for at least 15 days ending with the date of the meeting and at the meeting itself. If approval is to be given by written resolution the terms must be circulated with that resolution. Failure to comply with this requirement will not render the whole contract invalid but will render the fixed term provision void and the contract will instead be terminable on reasonable notice.

Once approved, copies of all directors' service contracts, other than those which have less than 12 months to run or are of an indefinite period and can be terminated by less than 12 months' notice, must be kept at the registered office or other place notified to the Registrar of Companies and must be open to inspection by members.

A director's remuneration will be taxable to income tax under Schedule E. The PAYE system will apply to such payments, obliging the company to deduct tax at source. The company will also be obliged to deduct employee's national insurance contributions and to pay the employer's contributions. Both the remuneration paid, provided it is wholly and exclusively incurred for the purposes of trade and is not otherwise prohibited by statute, and the employer's national insurance contributions, are deductible from the company's Schedule D I profits. Since the director will (unless he earns less than £8,500 p.a. and owns no more than 5% of the ordinary share capital) constitute a higher paid employee, any benefits in kind will be taxable either under the general rules for higher paid employees as a benefit provided (s 154 Income and Corporation Taxes Act 1988 on the cost incurred in providing the benefit (s 156(1)) or under specific statutory provisions (e.g. s 157 cars available for private use).

(d) Sale of Assets to or Purchase of Assets from Directors.

Section 320 Companies Act 1985 provides that a company cannot enter into an arrangement whereby a director or a person connected with him acquires a non-cash asset of the requisite value from the company, or the company itself acquires such an asset from such a person without first obtaining the approval of the members in general meeting by ordinary resolution. A non-cash asset is any property or interest in property other than cash and an asset is currently of the requisite value if :

- its value is at least £2,000 and that value is in excess of 10% of the company's asset value; *or*
- its value is in excess of £100,000.

The company's asset value is taken to be its net assets as shown in the accounts of the last accounting period. If there are no such accounts (e.g. the company is newly formed) then the amount of the company's called up share capital is taken.

If the transaction falls within the ambit of Section 320 but is not duly approved:

(a) the contract is voidable at the instance of the company; and

(b) the director himself and any other director who authorised the transaction is liable to account to the company for any gain he has made directly or indirectly from the transaction and to indemnify the company for any loss or damage it may have suffered.

(e) Loans to Directors

Section 330 Companies Act 1985 contains a general prohibition forbidding companies to make loans to or to guarantee or provide security in respect of loans given to directors.This prohibition is subject to a number of exceptions, such as loans of small amounts.

Even if a loan can validly be made, it may have adverse tax consequences, particularly where the company is close. In that event loans to participators (see p42 post) result in the company becoming liable to make a payment to the Revenue equivalent to the current rate of ACT. As the payment is not ACT, it cannot be deducted from MCT and is eventually forfeited if the loan is written off. If however the loan turns out to be a real loan and is eventually repaid by the director the tax paid is refunded .

(f) Gratuitous Payments on Retirement

If the board wishes to pay a "golden handshake" – a non-contractual and therefore gratuitous payment to a director on retirement, this cannot be done validly without first obtaining the approval of the members by ordinary resolution (s 312 Companies Act 1985). Such a payment is likely to be considered by the Revenue as a payment under a retirement benefits scheme (SP 13/91) and hence charged to tax unless approval can be obtained.

Shareholders' Meetings

A company is generally obliged, unless it has adopted the elective regime, to hold an annual general meeting in each calendar year. This rule is relaxed slightly in the early years of the company when as long as the first annual general meeting is held within 18 months of incorporation another need not be held in the year of incorporation or the following year, as the case may be. In any event no more than 15 months must elapse between one AGM and the next.

All other meetings of the members of the company are referred to as extraordinary general meetings and will be required whenever legislation or the Articles dictate that a particular power is beyond the ambit of the directors.

Calling a Meeting

The general power to call meetings lies with the directors, who in normal circumstances resolve at a board meeting to call a general meeting if and when they consider it is necessary.

Members holding not less than 10% of the paid up voting capital of the company can, however, requisition the directors to convene an EGM pursuant to Section 368 Companies Act 1985 by depositing a requisition in writing stating the objects of the meeting and signed by the requisitionists at the registered office. The directors are then obliged to convene a meeting within 21 days and will be deemed not to have done so if they convene the meeting for a date which is more than 28 days after the date of the notice. If the directors fail in this obligation, the requisitionists themselves, or any of them representing more than 50% of the total voting rights of all of them can convene a meeting to be held not later than three months after that date.

Table A adds to these statutory provisions by providing that on receiving such a requisition the directors must convene a meeting forthwith to be held not later than eight weeks after receipt of the requisition. This provision was initially inserted to deal with the possibility of the directors convening a meeting to be held at some distant date in the future, since the 28 days rule was not introduced until 1990. This provision is however now of little value other than to keep directors informed of their obligations in the Articles.

In order for a meeting to be valid an actual notice must be served on each member and a defined period of notice must be allowed.

(a) Actual Notice

To be valid the notice must state the date, time and place at which the meeting is to be held, give sufficient information regarding ordinary resolutions so that a member can decide whether to attend and vote, state the exact wording of all special resolutions and contain a proxy notice. In practice the full wording of all resolutions is given so that no dispute over sufficient information can arise at a later stage.

Notice of an annual general meeting must specify that it is an annual general meeting. Traditionally the meeting will deal with what is known as "ordinary business" – considering the company's accounts and their adoption, the election of directors, the appointment of auditors and their remuneration and the declaration of a dividend. Other business is traditionally referred to as "special business", but even ordinary business must be specified in accordance with the rules set out above.

(b) Period of Notice

In the case of an AGM this is at least 21 clear days, the word "clear" meaning that the date of service of the notice and the date of the meeting are ignored. This requirement can however be modified if all the members entitled to attend and vote are prepared to consent to shorter notice.

In the case of an EGM the required length of notice depends on the type of resolution to be considered. For an ordinary resolution or extraordinary resolution 14 clear days is required whereas if a special resolution or elective resolution is to be considered 21 clear days is required.

Again it is possible for the members to consent to shorter notice, but in this case only a majority in number of the members having a right to attend and vote holding not less than 95% in nominal value of the shares need consent.

Points to Watch

These provisions as to notice are mandatory in the sense that a provision of a company's Articles is void in so far as it provides for lesser notice periods (s 369 Companies Act 1985).

Notice to be valid must be given not only to all members but also to persons entitled to a share in consequence of death or bankruptcy and also to directors and auditors (Art 38 Table A).

NOTICE OF EGM

[ ] LIMITED

NOTICE IS HEREBY GIVEN that an Extraordinary General Meeting of the above named Company will be held at
on 199 at .m to consider and, if thought fit, pass the following Resolutions of which Resolutions numbered [ ] and [ ] will be proposed as **SPECIAL RESOLUTIONS** and Resolutions numbered [ ] and [ ] will be proposed as **ORDINARY RESOLUTIONS:-**

SPECIAL RESOLUTIONS

(1) "THAT [ ]."

(2) "THAT [ ]."

ORDINARY RESOLUTIONS

(3) "THAT [ ]."

(4) "THAT [ ]."

Dated 19

By Order of the Board

....

Secretary

Registered Office:

[

]

Note: A member who is entitled to attend and vote at the meeting convened by the above notice is entitled to appoint a proxy to attend and, on a poll vote, instead of him. A proxy need not be a member of the Company.

Conduct of Meetings

A quorum must be present if the resolutions of the meeting are to be valid. Table A provides that this is two persons entitled to vote, each being either a member, a proxy or a duly authorised representative of a corporate member. Directors are entitled to attend and speak even if they are not also members.

Resolutions are decided on a show of hands unless a poll is demanded. On a show of hands each member or duly authorised representative gets one vote: each person in entitled to one vote whatever the size of shareholding. In contrast, on a poll each member, authorised representative or proxy will have one vote for each share held. A member's right to call for a poll will be governed by the Articles subject to Section 373 Companies Act 1985. Article 46 Table A provides, *inter alia,* that a poll may be demanded by a member or members representing one-tenth of the voting capital and by the Chairman.

The majority of resolutions are either ordinary or special. In order to pass an ordinary resolution over 50% of votes must be in favour whereas to pass a special resolution a minimum of 75% of votes is required. Occasionally however, for example on resolving to put a company into voluntary liquidation, an extraordinary resolution will be required. This, like a special resolution requires 75% in favour. The requisite percentages referred to are of members attending the meeting and voting. There is, however, one exception to this rule: an elective resolution requires the unanimous consent of all members.

Type of resolution	*Notice requirement*	*% of members in favour*
Ordinary	EGM 14 clear days AGM 21 clear days	50 +
Special	21 clear days	75
Extraordinary	EGM 14 clear days AGM 21 clear days	75
Elective	21 clear days	100

In the event of an equal division the chairman has a casting vote and can therefore, if he so wishes, push an ordinary resolution through.

It is also possible for the shareholders to pass a resolution without holding a meeting by using the written resolution procedure (Art 53 Table A). To be valid such an instrument must be executed by or on behalf of each member entitled to attend and vote. Section 381B Companies Act 1985 provides that a copy of such a proposed written resolution must be sent to the company's auditors who have seven days from receipt to decide whether the resolution concerns them as auditors.

The resolution can go ahead if the auditors:

(a) notify the company that it does not concern them; *or*
(b) notify the company that despite the resolution concerning them it does not require consideration in a general meeting; *or*
(c) the seven day period passes without notification from them.

If however they give notice within the seven days that in their opinion the resolution should be considered by a general meeting, this must be done and a written resolution cannot be used. Proposals to relax these requirements are currently being considered.

Since companies are not legal persons in the physical sense they will need to appoint a human representative to attend a meeting for them if they are a member. Such a representative is known as a duly authorised representative and can vote both on a show of hands or a poll, and can count in a quorum.

If a member cannot attend a meeting he can appoint a proxy to attend and vote in his place. Articles 60 to 62 Table A provide for the formalities of appointment which include, *inter alia,* an obligation to deposit the instrument appointing the proxy within fixed time limits if the proxy is to be valid. Since a proxy cannot vote on a show of hands it is crucial that the proxy is also able to demand a poll (Art 46 Table A).

Correspondence

The company name must appear in legible characters in all business letters, notices and other official publications, bills of exchange, promissory notes, endorsements, cheques and orders for money or goods purporting to be signed by or on behalf of the company, bills or parcels, invoices, receipts and letters of credit. If the name is not stated, any director who signs any bill of exchange, promissory note, endorsement, cheque or order for money or goods is liable to a fine and personally liable thereon. Section 348 Companies Act 1985 also provides that the company name must be printed or affixed in a conspicuous position in easily legible letters outside every office or place in which its business is carried on. In all business letters and order forms the following must appear in legible characters:

(a) the company's place of registration and registered number;
(b) the address of the registered office; and if a statement is made as to share capital it must be a statement of paid up share capital.

If the company is a limited company exempt from the requirement to have the word "Limited" in its name a statement must be made to the effect that it is limited. In addition business letters must either state names of all directors (including full christian name or initial) or of none. This includes shadow directors (see p90 post). This rule is not breached if the name appears as part of the text of the letter or as the signatory.

Entering into Contracts on Behalf of the Company

Problems often arise when a single director seeks to bind the company to a contract.

It may well be that the board has specifically approved his entering into this particular contract or contracts of this type on behalf of the company, for example by appointing him as its authorised representative. By doing this the board has delegated its powers in this area to him. He will then have clear authority to enter into the contract and the company will automatically be bound.

It may be however that the director has not specifically been authorised to enter into such contracts. Nevertheless the company will still be bound if:

(a) It could be said that the express powers he has been given must imply the power to do something not specifically mentioned. For example, he is expressly appointed as sales manager to sell the cars of a car dealing company. It must necessarily be implied that his authorisation must include the ability to enter into contracts on behalf of the company to take used cars in part exchange.
(b) The company gives the impression to outsiders that the director has this power, often by appointing him to a particular position. As sales director, for example, outsiders will be entitled to assume that he has the power to enter into contracts to sell on behalf of the company.

If the director purports to have, but does not possess, any actual, implied, or apparent authority, then his actions will not bind the company and he will be personally liable to the third party concerned for breach of warranty of authority.

Authentication of Documents

(a) Documents Requiring Signature
Third parties will obviously be concerned, particularly when an important contract is involved, to ensure that the person purporting to sign the contract on behalf of the company is duly authorised to do so. In these circumstances it is common for third parties to request sight of board minutes approving the contract and specifically appointing the director concerned as signatory on behalf of the company.

(b) Documents Requiring Execution
Documents may be validly executed by signature of a director and a secretary or two directors (s 36A(4) Companies Act 1985) or, where a company has adopted a seal, by the affixing of the seal. Table A provides that such a seal may only be used by the authority of the directors or a committee authorised by them and that, unless the directors determine otherwise, the document to which the seal is affixed should be signed by a director and the company secretary or two directors.

Filing Requirements

The company is subject to a continuing obligation to observe formal filing requirements. In some cases this entails the despatch of forms or printed documents to the Registrar of Companies, in others the maintenance of records (internal filing requirements).

> ***Practical Tip***
> In order to ensure that all filing requirements are duly completed, it is suggested that these are set out in board minutes in detail as the procedural requirements are fulfilled (e.g. "The Secretary was instructed to file Form [ ] and to complete the Register of [ ]). A copy of such minutes can then be used as a checklist to ensure that all filing requirements have been completed.

1. Internal Filing Requirements

The Companies Act dictates that the following statutory books must be kept:

- Register of Members.
- Register of Directors.
- Register of Company Secretaries.
- Register of Directors' Interests in Shares and Debentures.
- Register of Charges over the Company's Assets.

The following must also be kept:

- Copies of written directors' service contracts and a written memorandum of any that are oral.
- Minute books – i.e. minutes of proceedings at general and directors' meetings. *Note:* when signed by the chairman of the meeting or of the next meeting such minutes act as prima facie evidence of the proceedings (s 382(2) Companies Act 1985).
- Accounting records.
- Copies of the Memorandum and Articles.

All of the above must be kept at the registered office except for the Register of Members, Register of Directors' Interests and directors' service contracts which can be kept elsewhere. The Registrar of Companies must however be notified if they are kept otherwise than at the registered office.

A number of companies also keep a Register of Transfers and a Register of Allotments. These are however purely optional.

Requirement to File Documents with the Registrar of Companies

A number of procedures require the submission of a form giving relevant details to the Registrar of Companies. In addition the following (either a printed copy or in another form approved by the Registrar of Companies) must be submitted to the Registrar within 15 days after it is passed or made:

- special resolution;
- extraordinary resolution;
- elective resolution;
- written resolution (if it would otherwise have required a special or extraordinary resolution).

Most ordinary resolutions do not require submission, but a number of exceptional ones do, the most common of which are:

- a resolution to revoke the elective regime;
- a resolution approving an increase in authorised share capital;
- a Section 80 resolution.

In the following cases a fee must be paid:

- Change of name (£20).
- Incorporation (£20).
- Annual return (£18).

Documents filed with the Registrar are placed on microfiche and are open to public inspection on payment of a small fee.

Annual Return

The directors of the company are required to make an annual return each year to the Registrar of Companies in the prescribed form, currently Form 363. This must be submitted within 28 days after the company's "return date", i.e. each anniversary of the company's incorporation.

The return must include the following:

- Address of registered office;
- Details of main business activities;
- Details of directors;
- Details of company secretary;
- Details of issued share capital;
- Details of changes in shareholdings in the return period;
- Details of any elective resolutions.

Form 363 represents an important summary of vital information relating to the company and is a valuable starting point when looking at a company search.

Accounting Records

The Companies Act 1985 imposes upon companies a continuing obligation to maintain accurate accounting records which are sufficient, *inter alia,* to show and explain the company's transactions and:

(a) disclose with reasonable accuracy, at any time, the financial position of the company at that time; *and*

(b) enable the directors to ensure that any balance sheet and profit and loss account prepared complies with the requirements of the Act.

In addition the company must prepare a set of annual accounts, comprising a balance sheet and profit and loss account for each of its financial years (such financial year being determined by the accounting reference date notified to the Registrar of Companies). These accounts must comply with the provisions of Schedule 4, which sets out detailed requirements as to precise contents.

The directors must also prepare a directors' report for each financial year. This must, *inter alia,* contain a fair review of the development of the business of the company during the financial year and of the position at the end of it. It must also state the amount (if any) which they recommend should be paid as dividend and the amount (if any) which they propose should be carried to reserves. The report must also comply with Schedule 4 in making certain declarations.

The annual accounts must be approved by the board of directors and signed, on the balance sheet, by a director on behalf of the board. The accounts must then be laid before the company in general meeting ("the accounts meeting"), when the auditor must make a report to the general meeting as to whether in his opinion the accounts have been properly prepared in accordance with the Act. The report must state in particular whether in the auditor's opinion they give a true and fair view as to the state of affairs of the company at the end of the financial year and of the profit or loss for the financial year. The accounts meeting can however be dispensed with under the elective regime (see p13 ante).

Whether or not the elective regime has been adopted, the company is also required to send copies of the accounts to all shareholders before the accounts meeting (if any) and in any event within 10 months of the end of the company's financial year. A copy of the accounts, the directors' report and auditors' report must be filed with the Registrar of Companies, and then become a matter of public record. The entire process of laying the accounts before the members and delivery of the accounts to the Registrar must take place within 10 months after the end of the accounting reference period unless the company is newly incorporated, in which case the period is within 10 months from the first anniversary of incorporation or three months from the end of the accounting reference period whichever is the later. In the case of "small" or "medium" sized companies the requirements are less stringent and, *inter alia,* an abbreviated form of accounts can be submitted and a full auditors' report is not required.

	Small company	*Medium sized company*
Turnover not exceeding:	£2.8 million	£11.2 million
Balance sheet total not more than:	£1.4 million	£5.6 million
Number of employees not more than:	50	35

The Taxation Treatment of Companies

Companies do not pay income tax, capital gains tax or inheritance tax. Instead they are subject to a tax on both their income and capital profits, corporation tax, and, subject to the current registration criteria (see p20 ante) will fall within the VAT regime.

Corporation tax rates look attractive at first sight when compared to those applicable to the income and capital profits of individuals. The rate is 33% for FY 1996. However, a "small company" with profits not exceeding £300,000, will pay corporation tax on its entire profits at the reduced rate of 24% (the "small companies rate").

It is of great significance to the individuals concerned that this tax charge lies within the company itself, a separate legal entity, and that attempts to put this profit into the hands of the owners of the company will themselves represent taxable events. Thus, if a company makes a trading profit it will pay corporation tax on those profits and if it then attempts to distribute them to its shareholders by way of dividend a further charge to tax will arise in the individuals' hands.

The tax year for companies runs from 1 April to 31 March and rates of corporation tax are fixed by reference to financial years, commonly referred to as "FY". The year when the FY begins is used as a description (e.g. the tax year running from 1 April 1996 to 31 March 1997 is referred to as FY 96).

The tax is assessed and charged on the profits of a company's accounting period. Since the majority of companies will not use an accounting period identical to the tax year in drawing up their accounts, profits are apportioned on a time basis to determine the appropriate rate.

1. Taxable Profits

The charge to tax is imposed on both income and capital profits whether or not such profits are distributed to shareholders. The figure actually chargeable to tax is calculated as follows:

1. Ascertain total income and capital profits (known as "total profits") using general calculation principles as for individuals. In the case of income this entails ascertaining income arising within each of the Schedules, and for capital gains an assessment of the net gains figure calculated on the usual consideration less base cost (as increased by indexation) figure.

Points to watch

The following differences from the treatment of individuals should however be noted:

(a) there are no income tax personal allowances for companies;
(b) there is no capital gains annual exemption for a company;
(c) charges on income are deducted from both capital and income profits.

2. Deduct any charges on income paid during the period.
3. Charge tax at the appropriate rate.

However, should the profits of the company exceed £300,000 but not to exceed £1,500,000, a marginal rate applies, the affect of which is that the rate applicable to the profits of the company will gradually rise to the 33% level.

Points to Watch

In calculating the company's income profits dividends received from UK resident companies are not taken into account. These payments, together with the ACT tax credit are known as "franked investment income" and are taken into account in calculating the rate of tax which applies.

Treatment of Taxable Profits

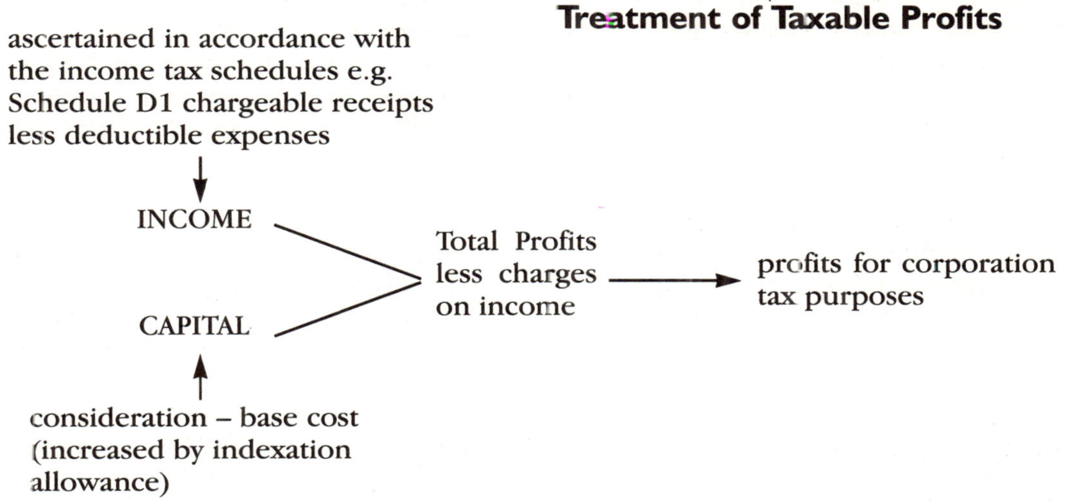

In the case of a trading company it is likely that the main source of income will be the trade itself and the majority of profits will therefore fall within Schedule DI. Schedule DI profits are calculated by taking chargeable receipts less deductible expenses and the following, provided they do not fall foul of the statutory rules concerning deductibility (e.g. that the sums should be wholly and exclusively incurred for the benefit of the trade – Section 74(1) Income and Corporation Taxes Act 1988) will usually be allowable as expenses:

- directors' fees;
- employees' salaries
- rent on business premises;
- interest on a bank overdraft;
- yearly interest* on loans from a UK bank (*i.e. the loan is capable of lasting for more than 12 months)

Charges on income, unlike deductible expenses, are deductible from all income and capital profits. The following are examples of such charges:

- interest payments to debenture holders other than UK banks;
- patent royalties;
- covenanted payments to charities.

Capital allowances may also be available on the purchase of certain capital assets such as plant and machinery and industrial buildings to reduce further the taxable profit. In the case of a company these are effectively treated as trading expenses of the accounting period.

Point to Watch
The payment of a dividend is neither a deductible expense nor a charge on income (i.e. it does not reduce profits chargeable to corporation tax).

2. Losses

Trading Losses

If the company makes a trading loss instead of a trading profit, the obvious consequence will be that no Schedule DI profit will arise in that period. In addition, the loss can be used to offset other tax liabilities in the following ways:

(a) the loss can be deducted from any profits, whether income or capital, of the same accounting period, hence further reducing the liability to corporation tax.

(b) if not completely absorbed by set-off against profits of the current accounting period, the loss can then be carried back against any profits of the 36 months preceding the accounting period in which the loss was incurred.

(c) as an alternative to or after using (a) and (b), the loss can be carried forward indefinitely and set against future income profits of the same trade (ss 393A and s 393 Income and Corporation Taxes Act 1988).

3. Payment of Tax

Since 1 October 1993 the payment of corporation tax has been governed by the pay and file system.

Pay

Within nine months from the end of the accounting period the company is obliged to make a payment of corporation tax to the Revenue, this being the amount which it estimates is due on the basis of the accounts. Interest is paid by the company from this date if an underpayment is made, and overpayments also attract interest.

File

The company must then forward a completed tax return and supporting accounts to its tax inspector within 12 months from the end of the accounting period or three months from the date on which the tax inspector requests the return, whichever is the later.

4. Close Companies

The basic rules of corporation tax are subject to a number of modifications where the company is a close company (a company controlled by five or fewer participators or participators who are directors).

The term "participator" basically means a shareholder, a loan creditor and certain other persons entitled to participate in the distributed income of the company. "Control" includes, *inter alia,* owning the majority of share capital or the majority of votes or the right to the majority of dividends. In assessing control the rights of the participator's "associates" (e.g. his spouse and children) are taken into account.

Main Consequences of Being a Close Company

- If the company is not trading it will be a "close investment holding company" and, *inter alia,* the small companies' rate will not apply.
- If the close company makes a transfer of value, it will be deemed to be a transfer of value by its shareholders who will bear the inheritance tax consequences accordingly.
- Any loan to a participator will give rise to a charge on the company (see p32 ante).

5. Dividends

There is no obligation on directors to recommend a dividend should profits arise in the company. A large number of small private companies where the directors are also the shareholders rarely if ever pay dividends but instead either retain profits within the business (hence increasing the capital value of the shares) or extract profits in the form of directors' salaries. Such payments have the advantage from the company's point of view of constituting deductible expenses for Schedule D Case 1 purposes (subject to their being excessive), hence reducing profits chargeable to corporation tax. The resulting national insurance obligations may undermine this advantage for companies paying at the full or marginal tax rate.

Should the directors feel that a dividend is appropriate they will be constrained by the following:

(a) A dividend can only be paid if and to the extent that accumulated realised profits exceed accumulated realised losses: Section 263 Companies Act 1985 (i.e. there are "profits available for the purpose"). This does not necessarily mean that a profit must have been made in the current year (although that may be commercially desirable) but rather that the figure for realised but undistributed profits over the life of the company is in excess of realised losses. It should be appreciated that while this rule is designed to ensure that the share capital of the company is maintained, it may still be commercially inappropriate to pay a dividend.

(b) Under Table A, declaration of a final dividend is placed within the ambit of the general meeting's powers, although they cannot declare a dividend in excess of that recommended by the directors.

Procedure

The following procedure applies in respect of dividends:

- Ascertain ability to pay dividend.
- Directors make recommendation at board meeting.
- Shareholders either approve recommendation and declare dividend, declare lesser dividend or decide not to declare.

Point to Watch

For corporation tax purposes a final dividend is treated as arising at the date it is declared. Any waivers should therefore occur before declaration.

In the shareholder's hands, the dividend will be taxed to income tax under Schedule F on the basis that 20% tax has been deducted at source. In the case of a higher rate tax payer a further 20% will therefore be payable. However, in the case of a lower rate payer and, somewhat unusually, a basic rate payer, no further tax will result.

CHAPTER 4

The Developmental Phase

CHAPTER 4

The Developmental Phase

As the solicitor's corporate client becomes more successful, a point will eventually be reached where further capital is required to fund continuing development.

Raising New Capital

The client's choice, in simple terms, is either to borrow money or to issue new shares. The limited availability of capital in the current economic climate may dictate the choice, but should the client be free to choose he must consider the respective characteristics of the two forms of investment in order to decide which is most suitable for the company.

Debt Characteristics

1. Defined investment time period – money is lent on the basis that it will be repaid at a fixed point in time.
2. Fixed return via an agreed interest rate.
3. Confers no right to vote at a shareholders meeting.
4. Does not directly benefit from appreciation of corporate assets.
5. Paid in priority to shareholders' capital on winding-up.
6. Payment of interest is deductible from company profits for tax purposes.

Share Capital: Characteristics

1. A permanent investment – no right to repayment of share capital.
2. Return via dividend not guaranteed.
3. Confers right to vote at shareholders meetings.
4. Benefits directly from appreciation of corporate assets.
5. On winding up paid after debts but if company is solvent entitled to remaining proportion of capital represented by size of equity interest.
6. Payment of a dividend is not deductible from profits for tax purposes.

The client must be aware that in practice sophisticated forms of investments often blur the distinctions and undermine these characteristics. A relatively common example is the redeemable cumulative preference share.

1. A company can issue redeemable shares, which are shares which it is agreed will eventually be bought back by the company provided the Articles so permit (e.g. Art 3 Table A) and at the time of issue the company has other share capital which is not of a redeemable nature. In the case of a private company that redemption can even be funded by capital provided that certain procedural requirements are met (see p73 post).
2. The shares can also carry a preferred right to dividend, which means that they may be entitled to a first fixed percentage of any dividend in accordance with the Articles.
3. Since despite **2.** a dividend cannot be paid if there are no profits available for the

purpose (see p42), the Articles may also provide that the dividend is cumulative i.e. if a dividend is not declared in an accounting period the right to that proportion of a dividend will take the first fixed percentage of any dividend in the following year followed by the fixed percentage which relates to that year.

CLIENT CHECKLIST

How long does the company require the capital injection?
Does the company plan to give a regular return on the investment?
Are existing members content to give new investors a share in management via voting rights at general meetings?
Are existing members content to give new investors a share in the appreciation of corporate assets?
Are existing members prepared to allow new investors to take in priority to them on an insolvent liquidation?

Restrictions on Raising Capital

In seeking new capital the client may turn to a number of sources ranging from banks and venture capitalists to existing members and contacts. The client should be made aware of the following restrictions:

1. A private company commits an offence if it offers shares or debentures to the public (s 81 Companies Act 1985). An offer to the public is made not only when there is an offer to the world at large but also when an offer is made to any section of the public (s 59 Companies Act).

   A number of exceptions are provided however by Section 60 Companies Act which states that an offer is not to be treated as made to the public if the offer or invitation can properly be regarded in all the circumstances as either:

   (a) not being calculated to result, directly or indirectly, in the shares or debentures becoming available for subscription or purchase by persons other than those receiving the offer or invitation; *or*

   (b) otherwise as being a domestic concern of the persons receiving and making it. It is further provided that an offer or invitation is to be regarded as being of domestic concern, unless the contrary is proved, if

      (i) it is made to an existing member, employee, a member of their family or a debentureholder; *or*

      (ii) it is to subscribe for shares or debentures to be held under an employee share scheme; *or*

      (iii) it falls within these exceptions (i.e. (i) or (ii)) and although it can be renounced it can only be renounced in favour of persons falling in (i) or to persons entitled to hold shares or debentures under the employee share scheme.

2. It is an offence to issue or cause to be issued an "investment advertisement" in the UK unless either the person so doing is an authorised person under the Financial Services Act 1986 or the advertisement has been approved by such an authorised person (s 57 Financial Services Act 1986).

   The term advertisement is defined extremely widely to include "every form of advertising" which includes not only written advertisements but also circulars, exhibitions, films, broadcasting etc. (s 207(2)). The only safe course is to assume that anything which can properly be called "advertising" will be covered.

The term "investment advertisement" is defined in Section 57(2) in such wide terms as to include the advertising of share or debentures in a private company. Such advertisements must therefore be approved by an authorised person unless they fall within the exemptions contained in Section 58. Section 58(3), which provides that the Secretary of State may make orders for the purposes of exempting advertisements which *inter alia* have a private character is of particular importance to private companies. A number of exemption orders have been made to date providing exemptions, e.g. for issues to existing members/creditors and advertisements issued in connection with employees' share schemes. There is no substitute for consulting the detail of exemption orders currently in force in each case.

Point to Watch
Some texts still refer to the fact that Sections 81,59 & 60 Companies Act will be repealed in full when Part V Financial Services Act comes into force. It has now been determined that Part V will never be brought into force and that these sections will remain in force for the purposes of the private limited company.

Issuing Shares

Having found a potential investor there are three basic matters which must be dealt with before new share capital can be issued:

(a) Is There Sufficient Unissued Authorised Share Capital?
If not, it will be necessary to increase the authorised share capital by ordinary resolution (s 121 Companies Act) and to notify the Registrar of such increase by completing and filing Form 123, a copy or print of the resolution and a printed copy of the amended memorandum within 15 days after the passing of the resolution.

(b) Is There a Valid Section 80 Authority Authorising the Directors to Effect Such an Issue?
Such authority may have either been given by ordinary resolution or be contained in the articles. To be valid that authorisation must state the maximum amount of relevant securities which can be allotted under it and the date on which it will expire which (subject to the elective regime) cannot be more than five years from its creation.

If no such authority is currently available, it will be necessary to pass an ordinary resolution at a general meeting to confer such authority. A copy or print of the resolution must then be filed with the Registrar within 15 days.

(c) What is the Impact of Section 89 Companies Act 1985?
Section 89 provides for pre-emption rights on the issue of shares for cash consideration. If the allotment is to be for cash it will therefore oblige the company to offer the shares to existing shareholders first in proportion to their existing shareholdings on no less favourable terms than it proposes offering to the outsiders. The outsider will only be able to be offered shares if existing shareholders refuse the offer or cannot afford to take up the shares.

Section 89 may have been varied or even completely excluded by the Articles of the company. If not, it will be necessary to remove its impact either by passing a special resolution to relax Section 89 (this removal can last for as long as any Section 80 authority which the company has) or by amending the Articles by special resolution.

Points to Watch
Section 89 only applies to issues for pure cash consideration. Its impact can therefore be undermined by accepting non-cash consideration (in whole or in part).

The effects of Section 89 can be circumvented by offering the shares in accordance with its provisions to shareholders who have already agreed to refuse their requisite proportion. This may prove time consuming because each shareholder has effectively 21 days to decide, since the offer must state a period of not less than 21 days during which it may be accepted and cannot be withdrawn before the end of that period.

3. Further Restrictions on Issue

1. The issues of shares must be in the best interests of the company otherwise the issue will constitute a breach of fiduciary duty (see p27 ante).
2. Shares cannot be issued at a discount (i.e. for a consideration less than their face value), but they can be issued partly paid, with part of the consideration paid on issue and the balance left "on call".
3. If shares are issued for a premium (i.e. for more than face value), the premium, although not strictly share capital, must be credited to a share premium account which must be maintained in the same way as share capital.
4. The company must not give financial assistance to a person who is acquiring or proposing to acquire shares in a company (s 151 Companies Act). The term "financial assistance" is very widely defined and could include for instance the company guaranteeing a loan to enable the prospective shareholder to buy the shares. A private company can provide such assistance in limited circumstances provided that it follows a strict procedure involving *inter alia* the passing of a special resolution and a declaration of solvency by the directors. This states basically that the company is solvent and will remain so for the next 12 months, and is supported by an auditors' report.
5. If, as is often the case when venture capitalists are involved, it is intended to create a separate class of shares for the new investor, it will be necessary to pass an ordinary resolution to approve the creation of the new class (Art 2 Table A), and any subsequent variation of the rights attached to any class of share will be governed by the procedural restrictions contained in Section 125 Companies Act.
6. Redeemable shares may be issued providing that the articles so permit (Art 3 Table A does).

Basic Procedure to Issue Shares for Cash

Board Meeting

1. Report proposal to issue shares.
2. Section 317 declaration if director is to receive shares.
3. resolve to call GM if any of the following are required:
- Section 121 resolution to increase authorised share capital;
- Section 80 resolution to give the directors authority;
- Section 95 resolution to disapply Section 89.

4. Adjourn board meeting.

General Meeting (on short notice)
pass resolutions:
- ordinary resolution Section 121;
- ordinary resolution Section 80;
- special resolution Section 95.

Board Meeting

5. Reconvene and report passing of resolutions.
6. Receive applications for shares.
7. Resolve to allot shares and receive consideration.
8. Instruct secretary to issue share certificates in due course and deal with other formalities.
9. Directors make Section 324 declaration if appropriate.
10. Close meeting.

Filing Requirements

Registrar of Companies
- Form 123
- Amended memorandum
- Form 88(2)
- Print of resolution

Internal Filing
- Register of Members
- Register of Directors' interests (if appropriate)
- Minutes

CHECKLIST OF ISSUES FOR NON-CASH CONSIDERATION

1. The directors must agree to accept such consideration – they are not bound to do so.
2. Consider Section 320 if a director is acquiring the shares.
3. Section 89 pre-emption provisions will not apply.
4. Form 88(2) must be filed if the agreement re the consideration is in writing and that agreement must be duly stamped. If the agreement has not been reduced to writing, Form 88(3) must be used and the form itself must be stamped.

4. Debentures

Point to Watch
The term "debenture" actually means a document creating or acknowledging indebtedness arising from a loan, in simple terms a loan agreement, and therefore although this term is often used to refer to a secured loan it covers all such loans both secured and unsecured.

A number of questions must be dealt with before any borrowing, whether from an institutionalised or small lender takes place:

(a) Does the Company Have the Power to Borrow?
If the company is a trading company it will have an implied power to borrow for the purposes of the trade (this power will be reasonably incidental to the trading object) and a company with the power to borrow also has an implied power to give security for the loan.

It is however preferable that such powers are set out expressly in the company's constitutional documents because despite the removal of the immediate problems resulting from the *ultra vires* issue as regards third parties (see p10 ante) lenders are loath to waste time and energy negotiating a loan only to find that one of the remaining consequences of the *ultra vires* doctrine – the right of a member to apply to the court for an injunction to restrain a proposed act outside the capacity of the company – can prevent the loan going ahead.

(b) How is the Power to be Exercised?
The articles will dictate whether and how the directors can exercise the power to borrow. Under the current Table A the power falls neatly within the general ambit of Article 70, but special articles may dictate, for instance, that the consent of the shareholders is required.

Points to Watch
The 1948 and 1980 versions of Table A dictated that the amount for the relevant period of monies borrowed or secured remaining undischarged could not without the previous sanction of the general meeting exceed the nominal amount of the share capital of the company. It is therefore imperative to check the Articles of the company concerned.

(c) Will Security be Required?
Security will be required, particularly if a bank or other large lender is involved. The lender will seek to obtain the right to sell certain assets of the company to satisfy his loan if the company fails to meet its obligations under the loan agreement. This right is commonly known as a charge, and can take two forms:

(i) Fixed Charge
This is a charge fixed on an asset. The lender has the right to sell that asset and recover the proceeds if the debtor defaults. Not surprisingly the asset subject to the charge cannot be sold without the consent of the lender.

(ii) Floating Charge
This form of charge is used when the assets which it is intended to charge are of a changeable nature, making the inability to sell which comes with a fixed charge inappropriate. Instead the charge "floats over" assets of a particular description owned at any one time by the company and only fixes upon them on crystallisation. This crystallisation is triggered when

winding up commences, a receiver is appointed by a court, a receiver is appointed by the lender under a power given by the debtor, the company ceases its business, or any event occurs which is specified as a crystallisation event in the loan documentation.

Will Personal Guarantees be Required?

A personal guarantee effectively provides that should the company be unable to pay its debt, the directors agree to assume personal liability. If such a guarantee is to be given the directors will have a Section 317 interest in the loan which must be declared. However, this also falls within an exception to Article 94 and therefore obtaining a quorum should not be a problem.

CHECKLIST OF STANDARD TERMS OF DEBENTURE DOCUMENTATION

1. Interest rate
2. Repayment date
3. Security:
   - fixed charge
   - floating charge
4. Specifying crystallisation events
5. Prohibition of later fixed charges ranking in priority to floating charge
6. Right to appoint receiver
7. Power of sale
8. Other powers of receiver

Procedure to Enter into a Debenture

Board meeting.

1. Report on proposal to enter into debenture
2. Record consideration of terms of debenture in particular any security.
3. Resolve to enter into debenture.
4. Instruct secretary to deal with formalities
5. Close meeting

Filing Registrar of Companies

- Form 395 and original charge document

Internal filing

- Minutes
- Register of Debentures

5. Formalities

It is the company's responsibility to register prescribed particulars of a charge with the Registrar of Companies within 21 days of the creation of the security (s 398 Companies Act). If the charge is a floating charge this should include particulars of any prohibition on later fixed charges. Effectively however since the major adverse consequences of failure to register fall on the lender, this responsibility is often assumed by the lender.

In addition, if a fixed charge is created over land then this must be registered at HM Land Registry or the Land Charges Department as appropriate if it is to bind a future purchaser (even if he has actual notice).

> ***Practical Tip***
> When registering a charge, it is necessary to file a completely corrected Form 395 within 21 days of the creation of the charge. Any error which is not a minor error will not be corrected by the Registrar but will be returned to the presentor. A corrected form must still be filed within 21 days of the creation of the charge. If outside this period, a court order for an extension of time will be necessary. Although applications for registration are dealt with as swiftly as possible by the Registrar, it is advisable to mark packages containing Form 395 and charge documents "Mortgage Section" and to take particular care in their drafting.

6. Repayment of the Loan

The lender will endorse receipt on the debenture. The director and secretary should then make a statutory declaration that the debt has been paid on Form 403a and this should be sent to the Registrar so that the register can be amended to show satisfaction. Finally, the entries made against any land at HM Land Registry or the Land Charges Registry should be removed.

Development by Acquisition

The directors may determine that the best way to develop the company is to acquire an existing business which can be run as part of, or in parallel to, the existing business. The purchase of such a business is normally effected by means of an agreement to transfer (commonly referred to as a "business transfer agreement") the terms of which will be negotiated at some length between the parties. This agreement will be followed, at least in the case of assets where a documentary transfer of legal title is required, by a formal transfer of such title.

The business transfer agreement will need to be carefully drafted to deal, *inter alia,* with the following:

1. Business Contracts

Since existing contracts of the business will have been entered into by the vendors and the purchasing company will not be a party to them, some form of mechanism will have to be devised to deal with the effective handing over of such contracts. Clearly the best solution is for such contracts to be novated, however, it is unlikely that all third parties with whom the business has contracted will be prepared to do so.

2. Employees

The contracts of the employees of the business will also have been made with the vendors. However the Transfer of Undertakings (Protection of Employment) Regulations 1981 (SI 1981/1794) should ensure that since the transfer constitutes a "relevant transfer" (reg 3(1)) the employees will be treated as if their contracts had always been with the purchasing company. This will inevitably create problems for the purchasing company if outstanding liabilities to employees exist and some form of indemnity cover will need to be provided.

3. Consents/Licences

Care must be taken to ensure that any requisite consents to the transfer (e.g. landlord's consent to assignment in the case of leasehold properties) are obtained and that provision is made to ensure that any licences, such as consumer credit licences, under which the business operates are renewed. Provision must be made to ensure the vendors' assistance in ensuring the continuity of the business.

4. Taxation

(a) Stamp Duty

The purchasing company will be liable to stamp duty at the rate of £1 per £100 or part thereof on the consideration for:

- *assets which are the subject of the business transfer agreement* (other than land, goods, wares or merchandise, stock or marketable securities, ships or non-UK property); *or*
- *assets, the title in which is transferred by written instrument.*

In the case of land or marketable securities the need for registration of title will ensure that transfer of title occurs in writing. In the case of goods, wares or merchandise where title can pass by delivery, stamp duty will not be payable on the consideration due for such assets provided that a written transfer is not used.

It should be noted that the following are classed as "goods, wares or merchandise".

- stock in trade;
- moveable plant or machinery;
- cash in hand;
- cash in a current bank account.

No stamp duty should, however, arise by reference to the consideration for the following will however be subject to stamp duty:

- goodwill;
- book debts;
- know-how;
- the benefit of pending contracts;
- cash in a deposit account.

It is quite common to transfer cash to current accounts to reduce the stamp duty payable and for book debts to be left with the vendor on the basis that he will use these to pay existing creditors of the business. Any liabilities which the company takes over will form part of the consideration for stamp duty purposes (s 57 Stamp Act 1891).

The purchaser will be required to submit Stamps Form 22 when submitting the agreement for stamping setting out a bona fide apportionment of the consideration amongst the various assets. Submission will not however be required and no stamp duty will arise if a certificate is inserted in the agreement to the effect that the transaction effected by the instrument does not form part of a larger transaction or series of transactions in respect of which the amount or value of the consideration exceeds £60,000. For these purposes any consideration attributable to goods, wares or merchandise can be ignored.

(b) Capital Gains Tax

The vendors will *prima facie* incur a liability to CGT on the sale of the business to the extent that it constitutes a disposal of chargeable assets. They can however postpone this by the use of Section 162 Taxation of Chargeable Gains Act 1992, which applies where an individual transfers a business to a company as a going concern, together with either all of the assets of the business or all of the assets excluding cash, in return wholly or partly in exchange for shares issued by the company to that person. This may well influence the way in which the vendors are prepared to structure the deal and conflict with the stamp duty considerations of the purchaser referred to above.

The vendors may alternatively seek to reduce their CGT liability by the use of retirement relief (if they are 50 or over or retiring on grounds of ill-health), reinvestment relief (where they reinvest the proceeds in qualifying investments within the prescribed period) or hold-over relief (if and to the extent that the sale is not taking place at full market value).

In the latter case it should be noted that the purchasing company will be required to consent formally to the relief since the corresponding effect is to lower the acquisition cost of the purchasing company, hence resulting in a greater gain than would otherwise arise when it eventually disposes of the assets. From the purchasing company's point of view it may be considered preferable to transfer appreciating assets into the ownership of individual shareholders/directors rather than the company itself to avoid the " double tax charge" (see p4 ante) which occurs when gains are made within the company and then transferred out to shareholders.

(c) Value Added Tax

The transfer of business if made by a taxable person will prima facie constitute a taxable supply for value added tax purposes. However it will not be treated as such provided that the transfer is of all or part of the business as a going concern, the purchaser intends to use the assets in the same kind of business and the purchaser is a taxable person or becomes one as a result of the transfer (VAT (General) Regulations 1985, SI 1985/886, reg 4). If part of the business is transferred this must be capable of separate operation if the relief is to apply.

Point to Watch
If a vendor of the business is to become involved in the purchasing company as a director or is connected with a director a Section 320 resolution will be required if assets are of the requisite value (see p31 ante).

It is of course always possible that the business is owned by a company and the shareholders of that company are not prepared to sell the business but would prefer to sell the company itself. Such a transfer effectively means that the purchasing company will acquire a continuing legal entity which itself has continuing obligations and liabilities. In the circumstances it is usual for the purchaser to insist on a lengthy acquisition agreement containing both warranties and indemnities designed to flush out any problems by means of disclosure prior to completion and to provide compensation should an undisclosed liability arise.

5. Appointing New Directors

The proposed development of the company may result in the need to appoint a new director, e.g. the new investor in shares may only be prepared to invest on the basis that he is also given a role in the management of the company.

A new director may be appointed in one of two ways:

(a) By the Board of Directors.
In this case the appointment only lasts until the next annual general meeting when the director must be reappointed by the general meeting if he is to remain in office.

(b) By the General Meeting.
No appointment can be made unless:

- The person has first been recommended by the directors;
- Notice of the intention to appoint containing the particulars which would, if the appointment were successful , be included in the company's Register of Directors, together with a notice of the proposed director's willingness to act, has been given to the company by a member entitled to attend and vote at the meeting not less than

14 and not more than 35 clear days before the date appointed for the meeting.

- Not less than 7 but not more than 28 clear days before the date appointed for the meeting, notice has been given to all persons entitled to receive notice of the meeting giving the particulars which would, if he were to be appointed, have to be included in the company's Register of Directors.

Only then can the meeting validly appoint the director by ordinary resolution.

Filing
Registrar of Companies
- Form 288a

Internal
- Register of Directors
- Register of Directors' interests (if appropriate).

6. Alteration of Objects

It may be felt necessary on expansion, either because of the remaining consequences of the *ultra vires* doctrine or for the sake of appearances, to alter the objects of the company.

This is possible by special resolution under Section 4 Companies Act 1985. It should be noted that holders of not less than 15% of the nominal value of the company's issued share capital or holders of not less than 15% of the company's debentures entitling the holders to object to such alteration may apply to the court within 21 days from the passing of the resolution for the alteration to be cancelled. A person who consented to or voted in favour of the alteration cannot so object.

Point to Watch
The filing requirements on alteration effectively allow for such an application to be made, i.e. the resolution and a printed copy of the altered memorandum must be delivered to the Registrar within 15 days from the end of the period for making such an application.

CHAPTER 5

Dealing with Disputes

CHAPTER 5

Dealing with Disputes

Clients come to their legal advisors with a variety of problems associated with how the company is being run. In order to deal with such matters and to give sensible practical advice the solicitor requires knowledge of the law and its development. There is only scope within this work to give a brief summary, and it is suggested that where this key knowledge requires further development, the solicitor refers to one of the texts referred to at Appendix A.

A common problem facing minority shareholders in a private company is that the company is controlled by the majority shareholders or shareholders who can exercise de facto control of the general meeting. The decision making processes in a company are governed by democratic principles. The decisions of the board of directors are made by a simple majority (see Art 88 Table A) and resolutions in the general meeting are passed by either ordinary or special resolutions. A minority shareholder, who may also be a director, can find himself outvoted on the board and in the general meeting and must generally live with this fact.

Although directors owe fiduciary duties to the company when exercising their powers, shareholders can normally vote in general meeting in whichever way they choose even if motivated by personal interest. The directors often commit an alleged wrong to the company which they are either lawfully entitled to do or are allowed to ask the general meeting to ratify. This area is a minefield for the minority shareholder who wishes to complain, as the courts have proved reluctant to come to his aid and have thrown up a number of barriers to prevent an effective remedy.

There are numerous possible scenarios where a minority shareholder is effectively ousted from the company. The general meeting may refuse to declare a dividend and instead choose to distribute profits by way of increased salaries to the controlling director/shareholders. The general meeting may resolve under Section 303 Companies Act 1985 to dismiss a director/shareholder from the board. The director/shareholder will therefore be effectively sidelined from the company's activities and participation in its profits. A remedy short of asking the court for a winding up order on the just and equitable ground under Section 122(1)(g) Insolvency Act 1986 has traditionally been unavailable to the aggrieved shareholder due to the common law rule in *Foss* v *Harbottle* (1843) 2 Hare 461.

Protection for the minority has been developed in certain specific situations both at common law and under statute. If a company resolves to alter its articles that alteration may be attacked by a minority unless the majority had acted "bona fide for the benefit of the company as a whole" *(Allen* v *Gold Reefs of West Africa Ltd* [1900] 1 Ch 656). The Companies Act 1985 provides the following limited protection in the form of procedural requirements:

i) An alteration of the Memorandum or Articles must be by special resolution rather than ordinary resolution (ss 4 and 9);
ii) Sections 125 and 127 provide for some protection of class rights;
iii) Section 459 now allows a shareholder to petition the court on the ground of unfair prejudice (see p60 post);
iv) Section 122 (i)(g) Insolvency Act 1986 provides the somewhat extreme remedy of petitioning the court to wind up the company on the just and equitable ground (see p86 post).

The Rule in *Foss* v *Harbottle*

Outside these protections, a minority's opportunities to ask the court for a remedy due to alleged misconduct by the controllers of the company are limited by the rule in *Foss* v

Harbottle. This rule consists of two branches:

1. If a wrong is done to a company the proper plaintiff is the company itself.
2. A company can only function effectively if the will of the majority is allowed to prevail.

The rule encapsulates the concept of majority rule both in the board room and the general meeting. In order to allow the company to function it is deemed necessary to prevent minority shareholders from bringing complaints every time the company acts in a way contrary to their wishes. On the other hand it is also necessary to provide some safeguards for the minority in case of abuse of power by the majority. These safeguards take the form of what are commonly referred to as the exceptions to the rule in *Foss* v *Harbottle.*

The Exceptions to the Rule in *Foss* v *Harbottle*

1. *Ultra vires* or Illegal Acts

A shareholder may prevent the company from acting in a manner which is *ultra vires* the company's objects clause or which is illegal. Acts governed by the *ultra vires* doctrine prior to the reforms of Companies Act 1989 are made specifically actionable by Section 35(2) Companies Act 1985. Following the 1989 amendment this exception is unlikely to be needed except in exceptional circumstances. The ability of a shareholder to prevent an illegal act by the company is unlikely to be encountered often in practice.

2. Individual Membership Right Denied

Where a shareholder has rights under the company's constitution (e.g. the right to vote in a general meeting) he has a right to protect his individual rights from infringement under Section 14 Companies Act 1985. It should be noted that not all rights conferred on the shareholder in the Articles can be enforced against the company. Any outsider rights conferred upon him in some capacity other than that of a shareholder, such as a solicitor, promoter, vendor of property or director, will not be enforceable. The limits of these shareholder rights are not clearly defined. Some "rights" have been enforced by the courts, others have not. It seems, *inter alia,* that the court will not enforce a shareholder's rights to demand a poll at a general meeting which the chairman allegedly incorrectly disallowed.

3. Special Procedure or Majority

If the Articles require a special majority or procedure to be followed and the company has ignored such requirement, the shareholder has the right to challenge such actions. If the shareholder was not allowed this right the company would be free to conduct all its business by ordinary resolution contrary to the Articles or the law.

Points to Watch
It should be noted at this point that exception (1) is a true exception to *Foss* v *Harbottle* in that if the controllers of the company decide to act *ultra vires* the company or illegally, a wrong is done to the company and therefore normally the company would be the correct plaintiff in an action to prevent such actions. A shareholder is in such circumstances permitted to bring a derivative action on behalf of the company. Exceptions (2) and (3) are not true exceptions as the wrong is being done to the shareholders' rights, not to the company. The shareholders are thus able to bring a personal action themselves, or a representative action on behalf of other shareholders, to protect their own rights.

4. Fraud on the Minority

This exception is a procedural device whereby shareholders are permitted to bring an action complaining of a "fraud" by the persons in control of the company. The action is normally a misnomer as the fraud complained of is usually against the company and the shareholder must show that the company is unable to bring an action itself to correct the wrong because the wrongdoers are in control and therefore preventing the company from bringing the action. The procedure adopted is a derivative action. The shareholder cannot complain of acts which would be valid if approved of or capable of ratification by an ordinary resolution in general meeting. The shareholder must show that a wrong has been done to the company and ask for relief on behalf of the company. He cannot bring an action based purely on the consequent diminution in value of his shareholding.

This exception has been the subject of a large amount of case law from which has arisen various difficult obstacles which may prevent the minority shareholder succeeding.

The meaning of fraud in this context is not clear. It is wider than common law deceit, and includes acts which are deemed incapable of ratification by the majority such as misappropriation of company property, an abuse of power by the directors in bad faith and self serving negligence. Other breaches of directors' duties have been held to be capable of ratification and therefore outside the exception. Examples would include an abuse of power exercised in good faith and negligence which is not self serving.

There is a substantial grey area where it is not clear whether an alleged wrong is ratifiable or not. A shareholder is therefore always taking a major risk in bringing such an action as the court may agree there has been a breach of duty but decide it is capable of ratification.

There is another major problem with this type of action in that the court will require that a prima facie case is made out by the plaintiff without a full trial. It is necessary to show that the alleged wrongdoers are in control of the company. This obviously includes *de jure* control, but the courts have decided it also includes *de facto* control although the exact meaning of this is unclear.

The minority shareholder will encounter problems in obtaining the necessary detailed inside information about the company to mount an action and the cost of bringing such an action is another major drawback. As long as the shareholder acts reasonably, in good faith and obtains the court's approval in advance, the court will usually order the company to indemnify him for costs incurred by him on its behalf.

For a detailed appraisal of the rule in *Foss* v *Harbottle* and its exceptions the reader should consult a major textbook (see Appendix A). The substantive and procedural problems with bringing such actions have made them uncommon in recent years. The advent of a far more user-friendly remedy for minority shareholders in the form of Section 459 Companies Act 1985 means that in years to come the derivative action may fall into almost total redundancy.

Section 459 Companies Act 1985

Even if a company proposed to act illegally in breach of shareholders' rights or in a clearly fraudulent manner, the intricacies of a century of case law have made the rule in *Foss* v *Harbottle* a legal maze. It is an area long regarded as in need of reform.

A shareholder wary of these problems could always petition the court under Section 122(1)(g) Insolvency Act 1986 for a winding up order. Short of this drastic action there has been a lack of an effective alternative remedy. Shareholders in public companies who feel prejudiced by the company's activities are better positioned than private company members because they are able to sell their shares and realise their investment with little problem. There is no ready market for private company shares, and even if a buyer can be found the price is unlikely to be favourable and there is likely to be a restrictive transfer article contained within the company's constitution.

Since 1980 there has been an alternative. Section 459 Companies Act 1985 (originally s 75 Companies Act 1980 replacing the unsatisfactory s 210 Companies Act 1948) is a practical and flexible alternative which is quickly becoming the only reasonable remedy for an aggrieved shareholder.

Section 459 provides:

"A member of a company may apply to the court by petition for an order under this Part on the ground that the company's affairs are being or have been conducted in a manner which is unfairly prejudicial to the interests of its members generally or some part of its members (including at least himself) or that any actual or proposed act or omission of the company (including an act or omission on its behalf) is or would be so prejudicial."

Under Section 461, if the petition is successful the court has wide discretionary powers to make such order as it thinks fit for giving relief.

Case law states that Section 459 can be used in circumstances where formerly a derivative action would have been used and that equivalent relief could be sought under the section, thereby using it to sidestep the problems of the rule in *Foss* v *Harbottle.*

Interlocutory Applications

Much of the reported case law under Section 459 is at the interlocutory stage. The section talks of acts or omissions or proposed acts or omissions of the company. The section therefore allows for an anticipatory application. Applications to strike out are common on the ground that the acts complained of do not satisfy Section 459 or where there has been an offer to buy out the petitioner's shareholding (the most common remedy awarded under such petitions). A letter before action pointing out unfair prejudice may be enough to convince the controllers of the company to make an offer to purchase the shares of the dissentient shareholder.

Unfairly Prejudicial Conduct To Interests of Members

"Unfairness" is looked at objectively. The test is in effect how a reasonable man would view the conduct complained of. There is no need to prove bad faith or malice. Prejudice can take many forms but is usually shown by establishing a significant diminution in value of the petitioner's shareholding.

The "interests of the members" are not restricted to legal rights under the company's constitution (as a s 14 action is). The use of the word "unfairly" allows the court to look at members' rights under the constitution but also to take account of members' legitimate expectations arising from agreements or understandings between the members themselves. Such an extension of the meaning of "interests" allows the court in quasi-partnership companies to consider members' expectations of participating in the management and profits of the company. It may be that if the company was formed as a quasi-partnership with such mutual understandings it would be likely to be unfairly prejudicial if one participant was excluded from the company's management, or if dividends were not declared when one of the participants was a shareholder only and received no salary on the understanding that dividends would be declared.

The following situations are examples of situations where the court has either held that there is or suggested that there may be unfairly prejudicial conduct to the interests of members:

1. Exclusion from management

This is one of the most common scenarios alleged. In a quasi-partnership company it is usually quite straightforward to show that it is a legitimate expectation of a shareholder that he should be a director and be involved in the management of the company.

2. Inadequate Dividends

A member who has contributed relatively substantial amounts of share capital in a company, especially a quasi-partnership company, may be able to claim that he has a legitimate interest which is being unfairly prejudiced if no dividends have been declared when funds have been available for this purpose. If the member in question is receiving no dividend whilst the other participators in the company are drawing directors' fees he will probably have grounds for complaint. Much will depend upon the understandings or agreements made when the member joined the company.

3. Excessive Remuneration

A member in any company is interested to ensure the company is run effectively and that profits become available for distribution to the participators. If the directors are receiving excessive remuneration this may have an affect on the company operating effectively and on the availability of money to be distributed to the members.

4. Dilution of Shareholding

In quasi-partnership companies there will often be an agreement that members will hold and continue to hold a particular proportion of the company's shares. The courts may readily find an agreement to retain this position and that any attempt to dilute a member's holding by transfer or allotment is likely to be prejudicial to his interests.

Other situations which may be seen by the court as unfairly prejudicial conduct but which have not yet been subject to clear unequivocal rulings would include the following:

1. Alteration of Articles

Even if consistent with Section 9 Companies Act 1985 and *Allen* v *Gold Reefs of West Africa* (see p58 ante).

2. Breach of Directors' Duties

This is at present unlikely to succeed as a director owes his fiduciary duties to the company not to the shareholders. It would seem necessary to show a specific reason why a member could claim to have a legitimate expectation that the directors will not breach their duties to the company and that if they do that it is unfairly prejudicial conduct.

3. Company Continuing to Trade at a Loss

Although the member has limited liability and seemingly no interest in the company if it is insolvent it is conceivable that continuing to trade at a loss could constitute unfair prejudice to the interests of the members.

Remedies Available under a Section 459 Petition

The court has a wide discretion to make such order as it sees fit. Section 461 lists a number of possible orders but is not exhaustive. These are:

(a) to regulate future conduct of the company;
(b) to restrain any act complained of;
(c) to authorise civil proceedings in the name of the company;

(d) to direct the purchase of any member's shares by other members or by the company.

An order to buy out the petitioning shareholder is by far the most common remedy awarded. In certain specific circumstances an order restraining a person from acting in the management of the company has been made.

Ordering the purchase of shares is usually regarded as the most fair way to deal with the dispute. If the participators in a company are not working together and there are serious problems it is a sensible solution for one of them to leave. It should be borne in mind that if this remedy is all the client wants or is likely to achieve, settling the matter without litigation may be in his best interests.

The Articles of Association, or separate shareholders' agreement if there is one, should be looked at in order to ascertain whether or not share purchase provisions exist which could be employed for the client. There is no point in considering a petition under Section 459 if an adequate remedy is available within the company's constitution or other agreement.

CHECKLIST

1. Who are the directors and members?
2. What are their respective positions and powers as regards the board meeting and the general meeting?
3. Is there a solution to the dispute contained within the articles or separate shareholders' agreement?
4. If this is not the case consider possible legal remedies.
5. Does the dispute fit within any of the exceptions to *Foss* v *Harbottle*. Such an action is fraught with legal difficulties and is likely to be expensive.
6. Often a more practical solution may be found under Section 459. Consider the types of conduct actionable under Section 459 such as:
   - exclusion from management
   - inadequate dividends
   - excessive remuneration
   - dilution of shareholding
7. What remedy does the client want and is it a practical goal? The client's expectations may be higher than the solution allows.

CHAPTER 6

Leaving The Company

CHAPTER 6

Leaving The Company

The solicitor may receive instructions from a director and/or shareholder who proposes to leave the company or indeed may receive instructions regarding such a departure from the company itself. Care must be taken to ensure that the professional conduct rules governing conflicts of interest are observed.

Directors

Voluntary departure
If a director wishes to leave the board (e.g. for retirement) all he needs to do is to call a board meeting on reasonable notice and resign at the meeting. Whenever a director leaves the company Form 288b must be sent to the Registrar of Companies. The company's statutory books (the Register of Directors and the Register of Directors' Interests if the director owns shares in the company) will require amendment.

Compulsory Departure

(a) Disqualification under Company Directors Disqualification Act 1986
If the court disqualifies a person from being involved in the management of a company he cannot continue to be a director without committing a criminal offence (see p90 post).

(b) Disqualification under the Articles
It is usual for the company's Articles to specify certain circumstances where directors are disqualified from remaining in post. The standard type of provision is Article 81 Table A, which states that a director shall vacate office in a number of situations including if he should become mentally ill or if he absents himself from board meetings without the other directors' consent for more than six consecutive months, and the directors resolve that his office be vacated.

(c) Retirement by Rotation under the Articles
Articles 73–80 Table A provide that the directors must retire by rotation. This operates in the following way. At the company's first annual general meeting, all the directors are required to retire from office but are automatically re-appointed unless a resolution to the contrary is passed by the members. At every subsequent AGM one-third of the directors subject to retirement by rotation (or a number as near to one-third as circumstances permit) shall retire. Managing directors and other executive directors are not subject to retirement by rotation. The other directors must take it in turn to retire and it is open to the members to resolve not to reappoint.

The provisions ensure that directors' tenure is always on the agenda at the AGM. In relatively small or quasi-partnership companies these provisions are usually regarded as irrelevant and the Articles accordingly are drafted to exclude retirement by rotation.

(d) Removal by the Members
Under Section 303 Companies Act 1985 the members may dismiss a director by an ordinary resolution. This right of the members cannot be excluded by the Articles or by any service contract of the director in question. A director can, however, bypass the risk of a Section 303

resolution quite legitimately by the insertion of a *Bushell* v *Faith* clause in the Articles. This special Article will give the director enhanced voting rights on a resolution to remove him from office. It will usually be expressed as giving a multiple of votes for each share owned sufficient to prevent the ordinary resolution being passed. Obviously the director will also need to be a shareholder to take advantage of such a clause. In order to give full protection to the director the enhanced voting rights should be extended to any resolution proposing to alter the *Bushell* v *Faith* clause.

Even if there is no *Bushell* v *Faith* clause in the articles a director can protect himself in other ways. He may have a fixed term service contract of several years. If this is the case and the members dismiss him he will *prima facie* be entitled to the salary for the period outstanding on his contract. This is likely to be a considerable sum of money for which the company will be liable, a factor which may persuade the members not to dismiss him. Much will depend on the reasons for wishing to dismiss the director and the terms of his service contract. If he is guilty of misconduct the contract may state that he forfeits his claim for breach of contract (wrongful dismissal).

A member wishing to propose a resolution to remove a director will need to ensure that a general meeting is called. A written resolution cannot be used for this purpose. The directors may not be willing to call a general meeting, but if the member owns at least 10% of the company's shares he can requisition an extraordinary general meeting (see p32 ante). If the company's AGM is due, a member owning at least 5% of the company's shares can alternatively ensure that his resolution to dismiss the director is placed on the AGM agenda. If the company has previously passed an elective resolution dispensing with the need for an AGM any member can request that one be held.

In order to propose the Section 303 resolution the member must give the company "special notice" by delivering a formal notice of his request at the registered office at least 28 days before the general meeting. If the date for the next general meeting has already been set the member will know the deadline for such special notice. If no date has been set the directors may attempt to avoid the Section 303 resolution by calling a general meeting before the 28 day period has elapsed. This will not help the directors as in such circumstances proper notice is deemed to have been given.

On receipt of the request on special notice the company must immediately inform the director in question. The director has the right to circulate a written statement to the members and to speak at the meeting even if he is not a shareholder.

If the meeting passes the Section 303 ordinary resolution the director is dismissed. As with all situations where a director leaves, Form 288b must be filed with the Registrar of Companies and the company's statutory books will require amendment (the Register of Directors and, if the director is a shareholder, the Register of Directors' Interests).

Shareholders

Most of the provisions dealing with a shareholder leaving the company assume that the shareholder is leaving voluntarily. It is possible though for the Articles to provide that the shares of a member should in certain events be transferable compulsorily to specified persons (*Borland's Trustee* v *Steel Bros* [1901] 1 Ch 279). This type of Article is rare in practice but valid if in the original Articles. If the majority shareholders pass a special resolution to alter the Articles to give them a power to expropriate the minority's shares such an alteration is void as not having been passed bona fide in the interests of the company (*Brown* v *British Abrasive Wheel* [1919] 1 Ch 290). In a take-over context the procedure laid down by Sections 428–430F Companies Act 1985 should be considered. This permits a take-over bidder whose bid is almost completely successful to acquire the remaining shares compulsorily.

1. Transfer of Shares

The simplest way in which a shareholder may leave the company is by transferring his shares. The transfer may be by way of a sale or a gift *inter vivos*. The death or bankruptcy of a shareholder gives rise to the transmission of shares dealt with below.

A shareholder's name will be on the company's Register of Members, and in order to transfer his shares it is necessary for the company to replace his name with that of the new shareholder. The company secretary will refuse to register the transfer unless the company receives a correctly completed stock transfer form (see s 1 Stock Transfer Act 1963)

(a) Procedure on Transfer

The procedure on transfer is as follows:

1. Transferor completes the stock transfer form.
2. Transferor gives the stock transfer form and share certificates to transferee and receives consideration if it is a sale.
3. The transferee ensures that the form is "properly stamped", i.e.:
   (a) in the case of a sale it must be stamped to show payment of *ad valorem* stamp duty. This is charged at the rate of 50p per £100 or part thereof on the sale of shares on the value of the consideration. Consideration for stamp duty purposes includes not only cash but also stock or marketable securities and debts or liabilities assumed.
   (b) in the case of a gift this means that the certificate on the reverse of the stock transfer form demonstrating exemption from duty must be duly completed.
4. Transferee sends the properly completed stock transfer form and the share certificates to the company.
5. Within two months the directors must register the transfer and send the transferee a new share certificate, unless the directors have power under the articles to refuse registration.

(b) Restrictions on Right to Transfer

Subject to a contrary provision in the articles, a shareholder has a right to transfer his shares to whomever he wishes and the transferee has a right to be registered. In the case of a private company some restriction on transfer is usual, designed to prevent a person considered undesirable in the opinion of the directors becoming a shareholder, or to ensure the present shareholders retain their current proportion of the company's shares.

Table A contains a restrictive transfer Article in Article 24. It is a very limited restriction as the directors can only refuse to register the transfer if it involves partly paid shares (rare in practice), fully paid shares over which the company has a lien (again rare in practice) or where the procedural points in Article 24 are not followed. It is therefore usual when a company is set up for a wider restriction to be inserted into the Articles. The client's interests and views should be considered before the company is set up so that an appropriate restrictive transfer Article can be inserted.

There is really no limit to the types of restriction the Articles can contain but the following are commonly found;

1. Directors may be given an absolute discretion to refuse to register a transfer of any shares without having to give a reason for such refusal. This type of restriction was included within Table A prior to Companies Act 1980. It should be noted that if the transfer is to be refused the directors must pass a board resolution by a simple majority to that effect. If the votes are equal the transfer must be registered as the resolution to refuse to register has not been passed. This is important to remember especially when the company has only two directors and the chairman's casting vote has been excluded. In such circumstances if one director is in favour and one against, the transfer must be registered as the resolution to refuse registration is not passed.

Points to Watch
If shares are sold but the transferee is not registered, the transferor holds the shares on trust for the transferee. There is no breach of contract unless the transferor guaranteed that registration would take place.

2. The Article may allow the directors to refuse registration to any transferee who is not a member of the company or a member of the transferor's family. This type of Article is useful in small family companies where it is desirable to prevent outsiders coming into the company.
3. The Article may give the company's other members pre-emption rights on transfer. If a shareholder wishes to sell his shares he must first offer them to the existing members in proportion to their current shareholdings. This has the two-fold effect of preventing outsiders coming into the company and ensuring the current shareholding proportions are maintained. Only if the other shareholders are unwilling or unable to purchase the shares can the outgoing shareholder sell them to someone else. The directors will usually be given an absolute discretion to refuse to register such person. The price for the shares under such a pre-exemption article will normally be stated as that fixed by the auditor.

Points to Watch
Where a restrictive transfer article exists, the directors must decide within two months of the application for registration whether or not to register the transfer. If notice of their decision is not made to transferee within this time the directors in default are liable to a fine: Section 183 Companies Act 1985.

2. Taxation Implications of a Transfer of Shares

A transfer of shares constitutes a disposal of a chargeable asset. It will therefore be necessary to calculate the gain made:

Calculation of gain	
Consideration	A
less initial expenditure subsequent expenditure incidental costs of disposal	B
less indexation (i.e. expenditure x indexation allowance)	C
=	
gain (loss)	D

The shareholder will be taxed on net gains in each tax year (chargeable gains – allowable losses = net gain), but in the case of an individual transfer, he will benefit from an annual exemption for capital gains tax purposes, currently £6,300 of net gains. Any remaining gain will be taxed as the top slice of his income.

> **Point to Watch**
> If the transfer is not made by way of bargain at arm's length (e.g. a gift or sale at undervalue) the Revenue will substitute market value at the date of disposal for the consideration figure.

The following reliefs may be available to reduce his liability.

(a) Retirement relief

This is available to an individual who is either:

- aged 50 for over; *or*
- is retiring on ground of ill health

if he makes a "material disposal".

In the case of shares in a company a disposal will be "material" if, for at least one year ending with the date of disposal, the individual satisfies the following conditions:

- the company is his personal company (i.e. he owns 5% or more of the voting rights), *and*
- he is a full time working director or employee (i.e. he works for substantially the whole of his time in the business).

The amount of relief which is available on such a material disposal will depend on two things:

- the proportion of the company's total chargeable assets which are chargeable business assets (since relief is only available on this proportion of the gain), *and*
- the period for which the two conditions referred to above have been fulfilled ("the qualifying period").

If the qualifying period is 10 years maximum relief will be available as follows:

- The first £250,000 ("the lower limit figure") gains will be fully exempt.
- 50% of the gain between £250,000 and £1,000,000 ("the higher limit figure") will be exempt.
- If the qualifying period is less than 10 years the limit figures are reduced proportionately
  e.g. 5 years qualifying period.
- The first £125,000 gains will be fully exempt (i.e. the lower limit figure = £250,000 x 5/10).
- 50% of the gain between £125,000 and £500,000 (the higher limit figure) will be exempt (i.e. £187,500).

> **Point to Watch**
> If the actual gain is less than the higher limit figure, only 50% of the gain between the lower limit figure and the actual gain benefits from the 50% exemption, for example:
>
> 5 years qualifying period. Gain = £145,000. The first £125,000 will be fully exempt and 50% of the gain between £125,000 and £145,000 (i.e. £10,000) will be exempt.

(b) Reinvestment Relief

This is available if and to the extent that gains on the disposal of any chargeable assets by an individual (and certain trustees) are reinvested in a "qualifying asset", basically ordinary shares in a trading company, within the "qualifying period" (i.e. the period beginning 12 months before the disposal and ending three years after). In that event the disposal consideration and consideration for the reinvestment are both reduced by whichever is the lower of:

- the chargeable gain on the disposal;
- the consideration for the reinvestment;
- the amount specified in the claim.

The effect of the relief is therefore that the charge on the gain is postponed.

(c) Holdover Relief
This is only available where:

- an individual makes a disposal otherwise than at arm's length;
- the donee is prepare to join in a joint-election to the effect that the relief applies; *and*
- the asset disposed of is a "business asset" (which definition includes, *inter alia,* shares in a trading company which is either unquoted or is the transferor's "personal company" – see retirement relief above).

The relief is only available on the proportion of the gain which reflects the proportion which the chargeable business assets of the company bear to its total chargeable assets.

The effect of the relief is that

- the amount of the gain charged on the transferor is reduced by the amount held over; *and*
- the amount of the consideration which the transferee would otherwise be treated as having acquired the asset for is reduced by the same amount.

This effectively means that the charge on the gain is postponed until the transferee then disposes of the shares.

> **Point to Watch**
> Reinvestment relief and handover relief only postpone the gain whereas retirement relief wipes it out.

3. Transmission of Shares

Transmission is the process by which shares automatically vest in the personal representatives (PRs) of a deceased shareholder or in the trustee in bankruptcy of a bankrupt shareholder. The PRs or the trustee are entitled to receive any dividends paid on the shares, but as they are not registered as members they cannot exercise the voting rights.

Once the PR or trustee has proved to the company his right to the shares (i.e. by production of grant of representation or court order) he may do one of two things:

1. He may elect to be registered as a member himself by sending a letter of request to the company. This is subject to the Articles. Article 30 Table A permits the PR or trustee to be registered as a member in this way. Once registered he can transfer the shares in the normal way by stock transfer form to a third party.
2. He may transfer the shares immediately to a third party by a stock transfer form without him having to be registered himself.

> **Point to Watch**
> A restrictive transfer Article cannot prevent the transmission of shares on death or bankruptcy but may permit the directors to refuse to register the PR or trustee or intended transferee as the new shareholder.

4. Buy Back of Shares by the Company

Once shares have been issued and paid for by the members the money produced constitutes the company's capital. Creditors will expect this fund to be available to meet the company's debts, and because the members' liability will be limited the capital sum should not be diminished. This is the doctrine of maintenance of share capital. One of the consequences of this doctrine is that once a member has purchased shares he cannot normally hand back his share certificates to the company and ask for his money back. The only way he can realise the value of his shares is to sell them.

The doctrine does not mean the money must be set aside as a guarantee for creditors just that it must not be returned to the members whilst the company is a going concern (if the company is wound up solvent he will get his money back). The capital may disappear due to commercial or trading losses: that cannot be prevented but it must not normally be returned to members during the company's lifetime.

Two major consequences flow from the maintenance of capital doctrine.

1. dividends may only be paid out of profits;
2. capital invested by the members cannot be returned to members. There are however two exceptions to this:
   (a) Sections 135–137 Companies Act 1985: capital may be paid back to the members if it is not required for the company's business. This requires a special resolution of the members and the approval of the court. This procedure is long and expensive and rare in practice.
   (b) the company may redeem redeemable shares under Section 159 or buy back ordinary shares under Section 162. This may reduce the company's capital but does not require the court's approval.

Until the Companies Act 1980 a company was unable to buy back its own shares. Now it can under Section 162 Companies Act 1985. It may be considered desirable to use company money to buy out a shareholder in a number of situations where the other members are unable or unwilling to purchase the shares themselves and they do not want an outsider to join the company. It is a useful option in buying out a dissentient shareholder or providing money to a deceased member's estate for the payment of inheritance tax.

The ability to buy back shares is particularly useful in small private companies. The procedure is as follows:

1. The Articles must permit a buy back of shares. This must be verified first (Art 35 Table A permits it).
2. The members must authorise the contract to purchase by a special resolution (the member whose shares are to be bought cannot vote in favour of the resolution).
3. The contract or a memorandum of its terms must be available for inspection at the registered office for 15 days before the general meeting and at the meeting itself. It must then be kept at the registered office for 10 years afterwards. (If the written resolution procedure is followed the contract or a memorandum of its terms must be sent to each member prior to his signing the written resolution).
4. The shares are purchased by the company and are cancelled.
5. Register of Members and Register of Director Interests (if member was also a director) are amended.
6. Within 28 days of the purchase Form 169 must be sent to the Registrar of Companies stating the number of shares involved, their nominal value and the date of purchase. The form is subject to Stamp Duty.

5. Redeemable Shares

Section 159 allows a company to issue redeemable shares if the articles permit it (Art 3 Table A does so). The company can only redeem shares if they are fully paid up and if the company has issued other shares which are not redeemable. A special Article will need to have been adopted setting out the terms and conditions of issue: for example the shares may be redeemable after a set period of time or at the option of the company. If such shares are redeemed they are effectively cancelled, which in theory reduces the company's issued capital.

The company can redeem shares by paying the member from distributable profits, the proceeds of a fresh issue of shares, or, if a private company from capital subject to certain safeguards. The rules for determining what funds are available to redeem shares are the same as those for determining what money is available to fund a buy back of ordinary shares.

6. Funds Available for Buy Back or Redemption

Generally the money may come from either:

- the company's distributable profits; *or*
- the proceeds of a specific fresh issue of shares made for the purpose.

Either way there will be no reduction in capital. If the purchase is financed by a fresh issue of shares, this fresh capital will replace the shares being purchased. If paid for out of profits it would seem *prima facie* there is a reduction in capital in that the shares are purchased then cancelled. In fact what must happen is that in addition to the profits being used to purchase the shares, a further sum of money from profits equal to the reduction in share capital must be transferred to the capital redemption reserve account. This is treated thereafter as part of the company's share capital. It should therefore be remembered that if for example profits are financing a buy back of shares at their nominal value the amount of money needed will be twice the share's nominal value. One half of the money is used to pay the shareholder and one half must enter the capital redemption reserve account.

Another option is open for private companies only: payment out of capital is permitted subject to certain formalities (see s 171) designed to protect creditors and members. If capital is to be used to finance the buy back a further procedure must be carried out in addition to the one detailed above. The articles must permit payment out of capital (Art 35 Table A does) and the company can only use capital in so far as there is a shortfall in available distributable profits and proceeds of any fresh issue of shares (the company need not consider a fresh issue of shares to fund the buy back). The difference between the two is the permissible capital payment.

Procedure for Buy Back Redemption out of Capital

The following procedure must be followed to authorise the purchase out of capital. It is in addition to that required for the approval of the purchase itself:

1. There must be a statutory declaration of solvency by the directors in Form 173 certifying that the company is solvent and will in their opinion remain solvent for at least one year following the declaration.
2. Form 173 must be accompanied by an auditor's report stating that the permissible capital payment has been correctly calculated and that the declaration of solvency is not unreasonable.
3. On the day of the declaration or within one week the members must pass a special resolution approving payment out of capital. The declaration and report must be available at the general meeting. Members whose shares are to be purchased may not vote on the resolution.
4. The special resolution must be filed with the Registrar of Companies within 15 days.
5. A notice of the special resolution must be published in the *Gazette* and a national

newspaper (or notice given to each creditor of the company) within one week of the resolution.

6. The declaration of solvency and auditor's report must be available at the company's registered office for five weeks after the special resolution for members and creditors to inspect.
7. A copy of the declaration and report must be sent to the Registrar of Companies within one week of the resolution.
8. The members and creditors have five weeks from the resolution to petition the court if they object to the payment out of capital.
9. If there is no such objection the purchase must occur between five and seven weeks after the resolution.

> **Point to Watch**
> If the company is wound up insolvent within a year of the declaration the recipient of the payment and the directors are liable for the amount of the buy back.

7. The Taxation Implications of a Buy Back of Shares

A buy back of shares *prima facie* constitutes a distribution by the company, and as such has basically the same consequences as a dividend in that:

- the company must pay ACT;
- the individual will be taxed to income tax under Schedule F in each case on the difference between the original issue price and the consideration for the buy back (see p43 ante).

However the buy back will *not* constitute a distribution if certain conditions are satisfied. Instead the gain will be taxed to capital gains tax in the shareholder's hands. These conditions, contained in Sections 219–224 Income and Corporation Taxes Act 1988, are complex, but can be summarised as follows:

(a) The Company
The company must be an unquoted trading company.

(b) The Shareholder
The shareholder must:

1. be an individual, personal representative or trustee.
2. be resident in the UK (ordinarily resident in the case of an individual).
3. satisfy a minimum period of ownership.
   (a) five years in the case of an individual or trustee
   (b) three years in the case of a personal representative (ownership by the deceased and personal representative).
4. be either disposing of all his shares or "substantially reducing" his shareholding.

(c) The Reason for Sale
This must be either:

1. wholly or mainly to benefit the trade; *or*
2. wholly or substantially the whole of the proceeds are to be used to pay inheritance tax liability arising on death and the inheritance tax cannot otherwise be paid without undue hardship and will be paid within two years of the death.

An application for clearance as to whether Section 219 applies or does not apply can be made to the Revenue and, provided all material facts are fully and accurately disclosed, is binding. In addition stamp duty will be payable on the actual return made to the Registrar of Companies on the buy back (i.e. Form 169)(s 66 Finance Act 1986) at the rate of 50p per £100 or part thereof.

Points to Consider

DIRECTOR OR SHAREHOLDER OR BOTH?

- If a director he may:
  resign
  be disqualified under Company Directors Disqualification Act 1986
  be disqualified under the articles
  retire by rotation under the articles and not be reappointed
  be removed by Section 303 ordinary resolution of the members.
- Whenever a director leaves a company, Form 288b must be filed with the Registrar of Companies and the company's statutory books will require updating.
- Shareholders will rarely be subject to articles providing for compulsory acquisition of their shares.
- Shareholders may leave the company by transferring their shares to another using a stock transfer form.
- It is common, especially with private companies, for the articles to contain some restrictions on the *prima facie* right to transfer shares to anyone.
- On the death or bankruptcy of a shareholder his shares automatically vest in his PRs or trustee in bankruptcy by way of transmission. The personal representative or trustee may choose to be registered as the new shareholder or transfer the shares to a third party without having been registered himself.
- In small private companies particularly the company may buy back the member's shares. This is particularly useful if a shareholder wishes to sell his shares, but the other shareholders are unable or unwilling to purchase them and they do not wish an outsider to become a shareholder.
- Shares may be bought back by the company using the company's distributable profits, the proceeds of a fresh issue of shares, or subject to certain safeguards, the company's capital itself.
- Whenever shares are transferred the company's statutory books will require amendment. There is no form to be filed with the Registrar of Companies.

CHAPTER 7

Corporate Insolvency

CHAPTER 7

Corporate Insolvency

A company may fail for any one of a myriad of reasons. Poor market conditions, poor management, important customers becoming insolvent leaving the company with bad debts, speculative ventures going wrong or a hundred other things can lead a company into a state of insolvency. Insolvency is defined as either the company's net assets being worth less than its net liabilities or the company being unable to pay its debts as they become due. These two situations mean different things, and it may be that although technically insolvent a company is still viable. Depending on the seriousness of the insolvency the company may be able to escape liquidation by way of informal or formal procedures or it may be that an immediate liquidation is the only option.

The law relating to insolvency is vast and growing all the time. It is beyond the scope of this publication to do any more than point out the various possible options open to an insolvent company and the advantages or pitfalls associated with each option. For detailed examinations one should consult one of the specialist insolvency law texts referred to at Appendix A. When advising an insolvent corporate client the legal adviser needs to know as much as possible about the company and may need to consult the company's accountant and/or an insolvency specialist to ensure that any advice given is not misconceived.

It may be that the company's current insolvent state is not serious or that it is likely to be only short term. In such circumstances there are legal mechanisms available to ensure that the company carries on trading and hopefully regains its former success. It may be that this is not possible and to advise a client to continue to trade when there is no reasonable prospect of avoiding an insolvent liquidation could lead to serious personal liability for those in control of the company.

It is proposed to give a brief outline of the principal insolvency procedures and to highlight certain important points, giving enough information for an adviser to understand the nature of the basic procedures and consequences of insolvency. The vast majority of law relating to insolvency is contained within the Insolvency Act 1986.

Insolvency Practitioners

Prior to the Insolvency Act 1986 there were virtually no requirements as to the qualifications of insolvency practitioners. This, to a certain extent, encouraged the rather unsavoury practice of "cowboy" liquidators or receivers being appointed, who sold off assets cheaply and often to the former controllers of the company in question. Those former controllers were allowed to set up a "phoenix" company carrying on the same business, frequently from the same premises as the first company.

The consequent lack of confidence in insolvency practitioners led to a system of licensing being introduced in 1986. The system requires that an individual may only act as an insolvency practitioner if authorised to do so by obtaining membership of certain recognised professional bodies or being authorised from a "competent authority". Most insolvency practitioners are solicitors or chartered accountants. The insolvency practitioner must be an individual, give security and not be disqualified from acting as such.

Only a qualified insolvency practitioner may act as a company's liquidator, administrator, administrative receiver or supervisor of a voluntary arrangement. There are no qualification requirements for non-administrative receivers, such as Law of Property Act receivers, court appointed receivers, or receivers appointed over company assets which do not form the whole or substantially the whole of the company's undertaking.

Arrangements

The directors of an insolvent company will usually wish to consider a plan to avoid a formal liquidation. They may believe the company can survive if its creditors are willing to show some flexibility. The directors may call the company's creditors together and suggest an arrangement between them and the company. It is possible that the unsecured creditors at least will be willing to accept a proposal which should lead them to realise more of their debt than they would upon a formal liquidation due to the necessary incidence of liquidator's costs.

The proposed arrangement may take any form. Usually a proposal will ask the creditors to consider accepting, say 30 pence in the pound, in full and final settlement of all the debts owed by the company. This type of offer may be combined with an injection of cash by the directors themselves to increase the dividend. The bitter pill of cutting their losses may be easier to swallow for the creditors if they are convinced that the directors are suffering financially too.

Another type of arrangement would involve a debt-equity swap. This means that the creditors exchange their debt for shares in the company. In order to persuade the creditors to accept this kind of proposal it will be necessary to show the company has some prospects. The creditors may agree to it only if the current directors resign.

An arrangement may include one or all of these suggestions or many more. Whatever proposal is made it will need to be realistic and persuasive. It may be that the creditors will only accept a large proportion of the overall debt owed to them but be willing to allow the company to spread payment over two or three years. From the company's point of view it is vital that any proposal made is practical. It is pointless to enter into an arrangement just to avoid liquidation if the terms of the arrangement make a liquidation more rather than less likely.

It may seem attractive to the directors to reach informal agreements with the company's creditors. This option is fraught with dangers as the creditors cannot be held to the agreement and may in any case petition for a winding up or seek some other method of debt enforcement. At common law it is possible for a company to enter into a formal arrangement with all its creditors in full and final satisfaction of their debts. This would be binding on the creditors. A formal procedure under the Companies Act 1985 or Insolvency Act 1986 will only be required if all the creditors do not agree to the arrangement. This is fairly common as there is often a proportion of creditors who will not be happy with the proposal whatever form it takes or will only be happy if the directors and the company suffer a compulsory liquidation.

There are essentially two statutory procedures available to an insolvent company short of liquidation. Either procedure may only be practical if the company is allowed a breathing space free from creditors enforcing their individual debts or petitioning for a compulsory liquidation. It may therefore be necessary to combine such an arrangement with an administration order (see p81 post) which allows for a moratorium on actions against the company as soon as a petition for the order is presented to the court. A proposal for an arrangement may not get out of the starting blocks if impatient creditors frustrate its purpose by debt enforcement before the proposal can be put before a meeting of creditors.

The two procedures are as follows:

- Schemes of Arrangement under Sections 425–427 Companies Act 1985
- Voluntary Arrangements under Part I of the Insolvency Act 1986.

The procedure for voluntary arrangements allows comparatively straightforward arrangements to be made between a company and its creditors and will be made binding upon the parties without the need to obtain the approval of the court. For more complex arrangements a scheme of arrangement provides an alternative procedure under which the court's approval is necessary.

1. Procedure for Schemes of Arrangement

1. Application to the court is made by originating summons. The applicant will usually be the company (i.e. by the directors), or the liquidator or administrator if the company is in liquidation or is subject to an administration order.
2. Meetings of creditors and members held to approve the scheme must be called under the directions of the court, and the applicant must decide what meetings are necessary. The court will only order meetings of those creditors and members whose rights are affected by the scheme.
3. The court settles the form of notice of the meetings to be sent to creditors and members. A statement explaining the effect of the scheme must be sent along with the notice of the meetings. The explanatory statement must also state what interests the directors of the company and (if the scheme affects loan security holders) the trustees under any trust deed covering the loan securities, have in the scheme, and the effect of the scheme on those interests.
4. Creditors and members entitled to vote at their respective meetings may do so in person or by proxy.
5. The scheme must be approved at the meetings by a composite resolution of both a simple majority in number and three quarters in value of those voting in person or by proxy.
6. If the scheme is approved by the requisite majorities, an application must then be made to the court to sanction the scheme. The court ensures its directions have been carried out and that the necessary resolutions have been correctly passed. It will then sanction or refuse the scheme. It cannot alter the scheme approved.
7. An office copy of the court's order sanctioning the scheme is delivered to the Registrar of Companies. It takes effect from this moment and binds all creditors and members of the company.

Points to Watch
A scheme does not bind anyone until the court has approved it. Therefore a creditor is not prevented from suing the company or levying execution on its property whilst a scheme is pending (unless the company is already in liquidation or is subject to an administration order).

2. Procedure for Voluntary Arrangements

1. The directors of the company will initiate this procedure unless the company is in liquidation or administration, in which case it will be either the liquidator or administrator.
2. If it is the directors they will approach a nominee, who must be an insolvency practitioner, to help in the proposal's implementation.
3. A proposal giving details of the intended arrangement is made by the directors to the nominee. It must contain a statement of affairs and explain why a voluntary arrangement is desirable and why the creditors might be expected to agree to it. It must also give details of any circumstances which might give rise, upon a liquidation, to a liquidator attacking transactions at an undervalue or preferences made by the company. In practical terms the proposal will need to be drafted by the directors and the insolvency practitioner together.
4. The nominee must, within 28 days, report to the court as to whether or not he feels the proposal should be considered by the company's creditors and members. This

report is not much more than a matter of record. The court will only become involved in the procedure if some problem arises.

5. If the proposal is being made by a liquidator or administrator who is intending to be the supervisor of the voluntary arrangement himself he need not make a report to the court.
6. The meetings of the creditors and members will then be held on at least 14 days notice.
7. The notice of the meetings must be accompanied by a copy of the proposal, the statement of affairs and the nominee's comments on the proposals.
8. At the creditors' meeting, any resolution approving or altering the arrangement must be passed by a majority greater than three-quarters in value of the creditors voting in person or by proxy. Any other resolution requires a majority in excess of one half in value of the creditors.
9. Resolutions at the members' meeting are passed by a simple majority.
10. At the creditors' meeting a resolution is not valid if those voting against it include more than half in value of creditors not connected with the company.
11. The arrangement cannot affect the rights of any secured or preferential creditor unless that creditor agrees to the variation.
12. The creditors' meeting will be the first to be held although they must both be held on the same day.
13. Once the arrangement is approved, it takes effect as if made by the company at the creditors' meeting. It is binding upon every person who had notice of, and was entitled to vote at the meeting.
14. The nominee will then become the supervisor of the voluntary arrangement and will implement its terms.
15. The chairman of the meetings (usually the nominee) must then report the result of the meetings to the court, the Registrar of Companies and to all those to whom notice of the meetings was given.
16. Appeal to the court is possible to prevent the arrangement's implementation on the grounds of unfair prejudice or material irregularity at the meeting.

Points to Watch
Although the procedure for voluntary arrangements is quicker and less cumbersome than that for a scheme of arrangement it suffers a similar weakness. Unless the proposal is made in conjunction with an administration order there is nothing to prevent a creditor levying execution against the company whilst the proposal is being drawn up.

Administration Orders

This procedure was introduced by Part II the Insolvency Act 1986. It was designed to assist insolvent companies in circumstances where there was no debenture holder able to appoint an administrative receiver. It was recognised that on many occasions the appointment of a receiver, rather than sounding the death knell for a company, actually enabled the company to trade through its insolvency and reappear leaner and fitter than before. Where no debenture existed enabling a receiver to be appointed, prior to 1986 there was no alternative to liquidation. Now a company can apply to the court for an administration order. It should be noted that an administration order and administrative receivership are mutually exclusive. They cannot both exist at the same time.

An administration order will only be a practical solution if there are enough assets in the company to pay for the comparatively high costs of the administration. Although initially quite popular the number of orders made by the courts has been reducing in recent years. This is partly due to the expense involved. The other main reason is that if a debenture holder is able to appoint an administrative receiver (see p83 post) this will normally be seen as more beneficial to the debenture holder than allowing an administration order to be made. Where there is an insolvent company it is usual for such a debenture holder to exist.

Procedure

1. The petition for an administration order is usually made by the company's directors.
2. The ground for the petition is that:
   (a) the company is, or is likely to become, unable to pay its debts; *and*
   (b) an administration order is likely to achieve one of the following:
      (i) the survival of the company and the whole or part of its undertaking as a going concern;
      (ii) the approval of a voluntary arrangement under Part I Insolvency Act 1986;
      (iii) the sanctioning by the court of a scheme of arrangement under Companies Act 1985;
      (iv) a more advantageous realisation of the company's assets than would be effected on a formal winding up.
3. The petition must be accompanied by an affidavit which must contain the following information:
   (a) statement of the company's financial position;
   (b) details of securities held by creditors and whether there is a power to appoint an administrative receiver (and whether such a receiver has been appointed);
   (c) details of any petition to wind up the company which is pending;
   (d) any other matters the petitioner believes may be of assistance to the court;
   (e) whether an independent report has been prepared for the company.
4. The independent report ((e) above) is of crucial importance. It will usually be prepared by the insolvency practitioner who it is intended will be the administrator, and it will need to conclude that the making of the order will be expedient. The court will rely heavily on the report.
5. A copy of the petition and affidavit must be served on, *inter alia,* any person who has appointed or is able to appoint an administrative receiver. Five days' notice before the return date must be given.
6. The presentation of the petition brings about an immediate moratorium on actions by creditors. No winding up resolution may be passed nor winding up order made. No security can be enforced against company property, no hire purchase goods can be repossessed, no execution or other legal process may be commenced or continued with and no distress may be levied without leave of the court.
7. A winding up petition may be presented to the court and an administrative receiver may be appointed.
8. If a winding up petition is presented it will usually be heard at the same time as the petition for the administration order. If one petition fails the other will usually succeed.
9. If an administrative receiver has been appointed by the time of the return date the petition must be dismissed unless the appointing debenture holder consents to the administration order. Such consent is unlikely to be forthcoming as most debenture holders will prefer to appoint their own administrative receiver whose primary duty is not to the company but to realise enough assets to pay off the debenture holder.

Points to Watch
It may be that the debenture holder in certain circumstances does not wish to be seen to pull the rug from under the company and may therefore permit the administration order to be made. Another practical consideration is the effect of the administration order's moratorium. It prevents a landlord levying distress. Distraint for unpaid rent survives the appointment of an administrative receiver. If the company's business is carried on from largely leasehold property the debenture holder's security would be subject to distress in administrative receivership. If an administration order is made distress will not be possible.

10. If the court is satisfied that the purpose or purposes specified in the petition are likely to be achieved it will make the order. The administrator appointed is deemed to be the agent of the company.
11. Once the order is made any administrative receiver must vacate office.
12. Whilst the order is in force no administrative receiver can be appointed and the moratorium on actions explained at point 6 *ante* continues.
13. The administrator has the same statutory powers listed in Schedule 1 Insolvency Act 1986 as an administrative receiver (e.g. to carry on company's business, to sell property, to appoint agents). He can remove and appoint directors and call meetings of creditors and members.
14. Property subject to a floating charge can be disposed of as if it were not subject to such security. The debenture holder's security is transferred to the proceeds of sale or substituted property representing the proceeds.
15. The administrator can dispose of other property subject to any other security with the consent of the court. The court will normally order that the proceeds of sale shall be applied in discharging the sum secured by the security.
16. Within three months of his appointment the administrator must send a statement of his proposal for achieving the purpose for which he was appointed to all the company's creditors.
17. A creditors' meeting is then called to approve or reject the proposal. If the proposal is approved by a simple majority in value of the unsecured creditors he will implement the proposal.
18. The administrator may apply to the court for the administration order to be discharged or varied if either the purpose for which it was made has been achieved or has proved incapable of achievement.

Points to Watch
An administration order has in theory many positive characteristics. The moratorium on actions allows the administrator time to turn the company around or consider a voluntary arrangement. But it is an expensive option, and also suffers from the weakness of being subject to an effective veto by a debenture holder.

Administrative Receivers

A debenture holder is a creditor of the company. If the debenture is unsecured he will have essentially two remedies if the company defaults under the debenture document. He may sue the company for the money owed and if successful obtain execution of the judgment debt.

Alternatively, if he is owed at least £750, he can petition for the winding up of the company (see p87 post). He will rank as an unsecured creditor in the liquidation.

If the debenture is secured, which is far more common, under the terms of the debenture the debenture holder will also have the power to appoint a receiver. If the debenture is very poorly drafted and therefore contains no power to appoint a receiver he can apply to the court for the appointment of a receiver. Nowadays court appointed receivers are extremely rare.

When lending a company money and taking security it is usual for the lender to take a fixed and floating charge over the entire undertaking of the company. The debenture document will expressly reserve a power to appoint a receiver should the company default on the terms of the debenture. An administrative receiver is a receiver and manager of the whole, or substantially the whole, of the company's undertaking appointed by the debenture holder with security over the whole or substantially the whole of the company's undertaking. The charge will cover *inter alia* the company's goodwill and this allows the receiver to take over and manage the company's business. This is why he is a receiver and manager. A receiver appointed over a lesser proportion of the company's assets is not an administrative receiver.

1. Appointment

Before an administrative receiver can be appointed the debenture holder must have formally demanded payment of the outstanding debt according to the terms of the debenture. It is usual for such loan facilities to be payable on demand.

Therefore following default under the debenture (e.g. two months' interest not paid) the debenture holder can formally demand payment of all the debt outstanding. The company will have only a few hours to pay the money, which it will invariably be unable to do, and the receiver can be appointed forthwith. The debenture will usually require the demand to be made in writing.

Once the demand has been served, the appointment is made in writing by the debenture holder. The appointment must be accepted by the receiver before the end of the next business day. The administrative receiver must notify the company itself, all known creditors, and the Registrar of Companies of his appointment.

2. Powers and Duties

The powers and duties of an administrative receiver will usually be expressly stated in the debenture document. Notwithstanding this he will have certain statutory powers unless these have been limited by the terms of the debenture. The administrative receiver will require the directors to submit a statement of affairs, and within three months of his appointment he must prepare a report dealing with the reasons for the company's failure, the conduct of the receivership, the amount payable to the debenture holder and the amount he predicts will be available for the other creditors. The report must be sent to various people including the creditors of the company and the Registrar of Companies. Within the three months he must also call a meeting of the unsecured creditors to consider the report.

The administrative receiver is an agent of the company. Although he owes some duties to the company, his primary objective is to realise enough of the charged assets to pay off the debenture holder. He must ensure that other creditors with priority over the debenture holder (fixed charges have priority over preferential creditors who in turn have priority over floating charges) are paid first.

He has similarly wide powers under Schedule 1 Insolvency Act 1986 to an administrator. He may of course carry on the company's business, get property in, dispose of property, borrow money, establish subsidiaries etc. Once the administrative receiver has recovered enough to pay off his debenture holder he may resign from office.

Points to Watch
A debenture holder has a choice of various remedies available to him. Unless there are unusual circumstances he will wish to appoint an administrative receiver. Such a receiver acts with the debenture holder's interests in mind. The administrative receiver is not court appointed and therefore the debenture holder chooses whom to appoint. It is a relatively quick and straightforward procedure. There is no need to involve the court and therefore the costs are kept relatively low. It is therefore unusual for a debenture holder capable of appointing an administrative receiver to allow an administration order to be made.

Liquidation

It may be that a company is so hopelessly insolvent that a rescue package is not possible. A voluntary arrangement and/or an administration order may have been tried and failed. Receivership may have left the company financially crippled, and in such situations, the only viable option may be to end the company's existence. Liquidation or winding up is the process by which the company's existence is brought to an end and its property is distributed to its creditors and/or members. A liquidator is appointed and it is his task to get the company's assets in, pay its debts if possible and to distribute any surplus between the members. Once this is done the company is dissolved and struck off the register.

It should be noted that not all liquidations stem from a state of insolvency. Many companies are wound up solvent in which circumstances the money left over after debts are paid is handed over to the members.

Although liquidation may seem a painful step for a company's participators to take it should be borne in mind that if a company continues to trade where there is no reasonable prospect of avoiding an insolvent winding up the participators may find themselves personally liable for wrongful trading or subject to disqualification proceedings (see p90 post).

There are three types of liquidation:

- members' voluntary
- creditors' voluntary
- compulsory

Note: The manner in which liquidators are appointed varies according to the mode of liquidation adopted, but once the liquidator is appointed his functions and powers are broadly the same irrespective of the manner in which he was appointed.

1. Commencement of Voluntary Liquidation

A voluntary winding up is commenced by the members passing a resolution in general meeting. The members' resolution may be:

Ordinary
On expiration of a set period of time or completion of particular adventure for which the company was specifically set up. This is rare in practice.

Special
This may be passed by the members at any time and for any reason. The reason need not be stated. This resolution will be used where the company is solvent and will lead to a members' voluntary liquidation.

Extraordinary
Where the company cannot by reason of its liabilities continue its business, and it is advisable

to wind it up. This resolution will be used where the company is insolvent and will lead to a creditors' voluntary liquidation.

Once the winding up resolution is passed the company ceases to carry on business except so far as is necessary for the beneficial winding up of the company.

2. Members' Voluntary Liquidation

In addition to the winding up resolution being passed by the members, the directors must make a declaration of solvency. The reason for this is that a members' voluntary liquidation should only occur where the company is solvent. As the creditors have no cause for concern if the company is solvent they have no say in the winding up. The directors will make a statutory declaration stating that the company is solvent and will be able to pay all its debts in full within 12 months. Any director who makes such a declaration without reasonable grounds commits a criminal offence. If all the company's debts are not paid in full within 12 months of the resolution to wind up, the directors are presumed not to have had reasonable grounds.

There will be no meeting of creditors. The members appoint the liquidator by ordinary resolution. He must be an insolvency practitioner. If the liquidator discovers the company is insolvent he must call a meeting of creditors within 28 days. The liquidation then continues as a creditors' voluntary liquidation.

3. Creditors' Voluntary Liquidation

There will be separate meetings of both creditors and members. Each meeting may nominate a liquidator. The members' meeting will occur first in time and if there is any disagreement as to the appointment the creditors' nominee will be appointed. Appointment of the liquidator is therefore effectively made by the creditors. The rationale for this is that because the company is insolvent, the members who will have limited liability have no further interest in the company. The creditors have the not inconsiderable interest of wishing to see as much of their debt paid as possible. If the creditors so wish they may form a liquidation committee which has certain rights to be kept informed of the conduct of the liquidation.

4. Compulsory Liquidation

Compulsory liquidation is where the company is wound up by order of the court. The usual court is the High Court, though if the company's share capital is below £120,000 the County Court has a concurrent jurisdiction.

The grounds upon which a petition for compulsory winding up may be based are listed under Section 122 Insolvency Act 1986:

(a) company so determines by special resolution;
(b) public company which does not obtain a Section 117 trading certificate;
(c) an old public company fails to re-register;
(d) the company does not commence business within a year from its incorporation or suspends its business for one year;
(e) if a public company the number of members falls below two;
(f) the company is unable to pay its debts;
(g) in the opinion of the courts it is just and equitable that the company be wound up, for example if the order is needed to protect minority shareholders from fraud or the order is needed because the company is a quasi-partnership and the participators have fallen out with one another and consequently the company can no longer function.

Persons Who May Petition: Section 124 Insolvency Act

- the company
- the directors
- a creditor or creditors
- the clerk of a magistrates court
- the Secretary of State for Trade and Industry
- the Official Receiver

The most common petition is made by a creditor of the company on the ground of the company being unable to pay its debts. There are three ways the creditor may establish this:

1. If a creditor is owed more than £750 he may serve a statutory notice in the prescribed form on the company demanding payment. If the demand is not complied with within three weeks there is a presumption that the company is unable to pay its debts.
2. If the creditor has obtained judgment against the company for a debt he is entitled to levy execution against the company's assets. If the execution on the judgment debt is returned unsatisfied in whole or in part, the company is again deemed to be unable to pay its debts.
3. Other satisfactory proof that the company is unable to pay its debts. This is a wide category and may be shown, for instance, where the company has many outstanding debts.

On hearing the petition the court has a wide discretion whether or not to make the winding up order, even if the grounds for the petition have been made out. In particular the court will consider the wishes of the other creditors. If a voluntary winding up has already been commenced it is unusual for the court to order a compulsory winding up.

If the winding up order is made, the Official Receiver becomes the liquidator initially. No action or proceedings may be commenced or continued with against the company except with leave of the court. The Official Receiver may require a statement of the company's affairs to be drawn up, usually by the directors. If the company has failed, he is under a duty to investigate the causes of the company's failure and its business dealings generally. He may report the findings of his investigation to the court.

Within 12 weeks of the date of the winding up order the Official Receiver must decide whether or not to call meetings of the company's creditors and members for the purpose of choosing a liquidator to replace him. If he decides not to summon the meetings he continues as liquidator. If the meetings are called and they appoint different liquidators, the creditors' choice takes priority.

Conduct of the Liquidation

Whichever mode of liquidation is adopted and however the liquidator is appointed the functions and powers of the liquidator are essentially the same. The company's assets do not vest in the liquidator but he takes over control of the company and is under a duty to take possession of the company property. He must realise the assets and distribute the proceeds in the statutory order of priority. Any money left over after paying off the company's liabilities is distributed among the members.

1. Order of Distribution of Assets

(a) Fixed Charges

A creditor with a fixed charge over company assets will usually enforce his security outside the liquidation. If the fixed charge is insufficient to pay off the creditor he will prove in the liquidation for the surplus as an unsecured creditor. If there is money left over above the amount of the fixed chargee's debt he must pay that surplus over to the liquidator.

(b) Expenses of the Winding Up
In a complicated liquidation these expenses can be considerable as they include the liquidator's fees and the general costs of the conduct of the liquidation.

(c) Preferential Debts
Preference is given to certain types of debt under statute (e.g. four months' arrears of wages per employee subject to an aggregate maximum; the previous 12 months of PAYE and NIC outstanding; the previous six months' VAT).

(d) Floating Charges
Floating charge holders therefore are only paid after the preferential creditors. There is often little money left for such creditors. They cannot gain priority as fixed charges even if the charge crystallised prior to the commencement of the winding up. Generally floating charges rank in order of date of creation.

(e) Unsecured Creditors
This will include normal trade creditors, business rates and taxes not within the preferential category. *Note:* A trade creditor who has supplied goods to the company may be able to claim the benefit of a retention of title clause in the contract of supply. If this is the case the liquidator cannot realise the goods in question for the benefit of the company. He must allow the creditor to take possession of them.

(f) Members
Any surplus after the above have been paid out is distributed between the members.

Once the liquidator has distributed the assets he will inform the Registrar of Companies that the liquidation is complete and the company will be formally dissolved three months later. If it is a voluntary winding up he must first call a meeting of the members (if members' winding up) or separate meetings of the creditors and members (if creditors' winding up) to which he will produce his final return and accounts.

2. Powers of Liquidator to Swell Company Assets

The liquidator is under a duty to maximise the assets available for distribution among the creditors. He has various powers available to him which he may exercise to increase or swell the company's assets or minimise existing liabilities. The most important of such powers are detailed below.

(a) Disclaimer of Onerous Property Sections 178 and 179 Insolvency Act 1986
The company's assets may include onerous property, for example a long lease with burdensome covenants or unprofitable trade contracts. The liquidator may disclaim such property, which will bring to an end the company's liabilities in respect of it. A person suffering loss due to the disclaimer can prove in the liquidation, but only as an unsecured creditor.

There is no time limit within which the power to disclaim must be exercised. An interested third party may force the liquidator to decide whether or not he is going to disclaim by serving written notice on him. If he does not decide within 28 days he loses the subsequent power to disclaim.

(b) Transactions at an Undervalue: Section 238 Insolvency Act 1986
On application by the liquidator the court may avoid a transaction at an undervalue entered

into by the company within two years of the commencement of the winding up. A compulsory winding up commences upon presentation of the petition. A voluntary winding up commences on the passing of the resolution. A transaction will be entered into at an undervalue if either the company receives no consideration or significantly less consideration that it provides. The company must have been insolvent at the date of the transaction. If the transaction is in favour of a person connected with the company, the company is presumed to have been insolvent at the time. The transaction will not be avoided if it was entered into in good faith for the purpose of carrying on the company's business, and at the time there were reasonable grounds for believing that the transaction would benefit the company. Discounts offered in the ordinary course of business would therefore be safe from attack.

(c) Preferences: Section 239 Insolvency Act 1986
A preference occurs where a company does anything which in the event of an insolvent winding up has the effect of putting a creditor or surety in a better position than he would otherwise have been in. The liquidator must prove to the court that the creditor or surety has been placed in a preferred position. The difficulty the liquidator will have is that he must also prove that the company was influenced by a desire to prefer the creditor or surety. If the preference is in favour of a person connected to the company, the requisite desire is presumed. The period for which the preference must have been entered into is six months prior to the commencement of winding up. This period is extended to two years if it was in favour of a person connected to the company. The company must have been insolvent at the time of the preference. There is no presumption of insolvency even if the preference favoured a connected person.

(d) Transactions Defrauding Creditors: Section 423 Insolvency Act 1986
The liquidator, *inter alios,* may apply to the court to set aside a transaction entered into with the intention of defeating the claims of the company's creditors. There is no time limit for such actions, and the company need not be insolvent at the time. It must be shown that the company has entered into a transaction at an undervalue (defined as in s 238 above) but also that the transaction was entered into either for the purpose of putting assets beyond the reach of present or prospective creditors, or for the purpose of prejudicing the interests of such persons.

(e) Invalidation of Floating Charges: Section 245 Insolvency Act 1986
Any fixed or floating charge created by the company must be registered at Companies House within 21 days otherwise it is void against the liquidator. Apart from this the liquidator usually takes the company's assets subject to such charges. It may be possible to attack such charges as preferences. Another possibility open to the liquidator is to attack a floating charge (not a fixed charge) under Section 245.

A floating charge will be void against the liquidator if it was created within 12 months prior to the commencement of winding up unless the company was solvent at the time or the company received benefit after the creation of the charge. The charge will therefore be an invalid security for any debts outstanding prior to the execution of the charge. It will only be valid security for a fresh advance of money made at the same time as or after the creation of the charge.

Therefore if the company is insolvent and owes a creditor money, a floating charge is executed to secure this pre-existing indebtedness and the company enters liquidation within 12 months, the floating charge will be void as against the liquidator. If the floating charge is in favour of a person connected to the company the time period is extended to two years and there is no need to prove the company was insolvent at the time.

(f) Fraudulent Trading: Section 213 Insolvency Act 1986
Fraudulent trading has been said to occur where a company carries on business and incurs debts at a time when to the knowledge of the directors there is no reasonable prospect of the

debts being paid. It involves actual dishonesty such as commercial men would regard as imputing real moral blame. If the liquidator can convince the court that the directors are liable for fraudulent trading the court will order the directors to make a contribution to the company's assets.

Due to the difficulties of proving the necessary state of mind of the directors liquidators tend to bring such actions only in very clear cut cases. *Note:* Fraudulent trading is also a criminal offence (s 458 Companies Act 1985).

(g) Wrongful Trading: Section 214 Insolvency Act 1986

Due to the problems of proving fraudulent trading, the alternative remedy of wrongful trading for liquidators was introduced. If the liquidator can establish wrongful trading the court will order the director to make a contribution to the company's assets. The amount of the contribution will be calculated as the amount of loss caused to the company due to the director's decision to continue to trade when the company should have ceased.

The action can only be brought against a director of an insolvent company. He will be liable if he knew or ought to have realised that there was no reasonable prospect of the company avoiding an insolvent liquidation and, from that moment in time, he did not take every step to minimise potential loss to creditors. Therefore once a director realises the company has little chance of avoiding an insolvent liquidation he must not be blind to this and allow the company to continue to trade at a loss. Some decisive action is necessary. He should at least gain advice from his professional adviser and follow that advice. This will usually involve taking steps immediately to put the company into liquidation.

The director will be judged both objectively and subjectively. He will be deemed to have the knowledge, skill and experience expected of a person carrying out his function in that particular company. If he had some special qualities such as being a qualified accountant he will be judged subjectively and the court will expect him to show a greater degree of skill and knowledge.

Wrongful trading applies to directors and shadow directors. A shadow director, as defined in Section 251, means a person in accordance with whose directions or instructions the directors of the company are accustomed to act. It does not include professional advisors. Banks and other institutional lenders have been concerned that their activities in laying down conditions for continued financial support to debtor corporate clients may constitute the lender a shadow director of such company and therefore leave the lender open to potential wrongful trading claims. The High Court has recently decided that in such circumstances the lender will not normally be regarded as a shadow director as all it is doing is acting in an appropriate manner to protect its security (see *Re PFTZM Ltd* [1995] BCC 280).

Parent companies and/or its directors may in certain circumstances be constituted shadow directors or subsidiary companies (see *Re Hydrodan (Corby) Ltd* [1994] BCC 161).

Although the threat of wrongful trading is a real weapon in the liquidator's armoury, the liquidator must be careful not to lay himself open to personal liability. The affect of *Re MC Bacon Ltd (No 2)* [1990] BCC 430) is that if a liquidator brings a wrongful trading action and fails, he is unable to claim the costs of the unsuccessful action as expenses of the winding up. Unless the liquidator is certain to win or has an indemnity as to costs from creditors he may be reluctant to bring an action. It may be more realistic to reach a compromise with the director in question.

Points to Watch: Company Directors Disqualification Act 1986

It should be noted that in addition to owing a company common law and fiduciary duties and being potentially liable for fraudulent and wrongful trading, an erring director or shadow director may find himself being disqualified from acting as a director. If a person is disqualified under Company Directors Disqualification Act 1986 he cannot take part in the management of a company without committing a criminal offence. The Act lists various grounds for disqualification some of which overlap:

- On conviction of an indictable offence in connection with the conduct of the company (s 2)
- Persistent breaches of companies legislation (s 3)
- On conviction for fraud in connection with a company (s 4)
- Persistent failures to make returns to the Registrar of Companies (s 5)
- On being found liable for wrongful or fraudulent trading (s 10)
- Undischarged bankrupts are automatically disqualified (s 11)

In addition to these Section 6 contains the most common ground for disqualification. The court will disqualify a person if he is found to be unfit to be a director of a company. A liquidator, administrator or administrative receiver is under a duty to report to the Secretary of State in respect of any present or past director of a company with which he has been dealing and who appears unfit to be a director. The Secretary of State will then take action to disqualify the director it if is deemed appropriate as in the public interest. The disqualification order made by the court will be for 2–15 years. Schedule 1 of the Act lists the type of conduct the court will take account of in deciding whether a person is unfit to act as a director. This list is not exhaustive. It includes breach of duty, misapplication of company property, the responsibility of the director for the company failing, the responsibility of the director for failing to provide goods or services paid for in advance and the responsibility of the director for failing to keep proper records and make returns to the Registrar of Companies. The court also takes account of the director's responsibility for allowing the company to continue to trade whilst insolvent and to trade using Crown money (e.g. PAYE tax or VAT).

Points to Consider

- If the company is insolvent, gather as much information about the company as is possible. Without the full picture it will be difficult to give proper advice.
- How insolvent is the company?
- Is it serious? Is it likely to be a short term problem only?
- Consider the viability of entering into an arrangement with the creditors.
- Is an informal arrangement feasible?
- Consider voluntary arrangements and schemes of arrangement.
- Bear in mind their inherent weakness of not being binding on creditors until formally approved.
- It may be advisable to combine the arrangement with an administration order to take advantage of the moratorium on actions.
- The administration order may be appropriate to enable the company to survive intact or for part of its business only to continue. It may lead to a more advantageous realisation of the company's assets than could be achieved on a formal winding up.
- The administration order will probably not be a practical proposition if an administrative receiver is in office or if a debenture holder has the power to appoint an administrative receiver.
- The administration order is an expensive option. It will usually only be a practical solution if the company has substantial assets.
- A company in financial trouble will commonly have borrowed money on the security of a fixed and floating charge over the whole or substantially the whole of the company's undertaking.
- Default under such a debenture will allow the lender to appoint an administrative receiver.

- Many companies survive receivership but it is more common for the company to drift into liquidation after the receiver has realised sufficient assets to pay off the debenture holder who has appointed him.
- The company's insolvency may be so serious that a rescue package is out of the question and that liquidation of the company is the inevitable and only option.
- The liquidation may be voluntary or compulsory. The way in which the liquidator is appointed will differ but his essential functions will be the same.
- The liquidator realises the assets and pays off the creditors under the statutory order for distribution as best he can.
- The company will be dissolved once the liquidation is complete.
- The liquidator has power to disclaim onerous property and to swell the company's assets by applying to court to upset certain types of transactions entered into by the company whilst it was a going concern.
- Directors of insolvent companies should be made aware of their potential personal liability if they permit the company to continue to trade whilst insolvent. Actions for wrongful trading, fraudulent trading and disqualification proceedings are a real risk.

PART II
THE NEW PARTNERSHIP CLIENT

CHAPTER 8

Setting Up A Partnership

CHAPTER 8

Setting Up A Partnership

Having taken the decision to run their business under the auspices of a partnership rather than via the medium of a company, the solicitor's clients will then require advice as to the requisite formalities. The solicitor should be prepared, *inter alia* to advise on:

- The date of commencement;
- The use of a partnership agreement;
- The regulations relating to partnership names;
- Partnership VAT registration;
- The proposed financial structure.

Date of commencement

Since the term partnership describes a relationship rather than a separate legal entity, it is not surprising that a partnership commences whenever that relationship itself commences (i.e. "the relation ... between persons carrying on a business in common with a view of profit" – s 1 Partnership Act 1890). The clients may well find that they are already in a partnership relationship and are therefore subject to the implied statutory rules contained in the Partnership Act. Any statement of a commencement date in a supervening partnership agreement cannot alter this fact. Since the implied rules are likely to be unsatisfactory (see p97 post) it is essential that in these circumstances a partnership agreement is prepared and agreed at the earliest opportunity.

Partnership agreement

The Partnership Act 1890 provides a set of rules which, in the absence of contrary provision, govern the relationship between partners. Although perhaps suited to the partnership of the late 19th century, these rules are hardly appropriate to the needs of a modern commercial entity.

In order to disapply those statutory rules which are inappropriate to his clients' needs, the solicitor will therefore advise that a detailed written partnership agreement should be prepared. If well drafted this will:

- Provide a complete statement of the rules governing the conduct of partners *inter se; and*
- Reduce the prospect of future disputes within the partnership by anticipating areas where problems may arise and providing for settlement mechanisms.

The consideration of these issues will also have the advantage of focusing the minds of the clients on the respective rights and obligations governing their relationship.

There is no legal obligation to have a partnership agreement, but the reasons referred to above provide a cogent argument for its use. In addition there is no general obligation for any agreement to be in writing. This is however preferable for evidential purposes and may be necessary when partnership property comprises land (see *Lindley & Banks on Partnership* Chapter 7).

It should be noted that in the absence of evidence of any agreement, all the courts will be prepared to do is to imply into the agreement such terms as are necessary to give business efficacy to the relationship: *Miles* v *Clarke* [1973] 1 WLR 537.

CHECKLIST OF IMPLIED PARTNERSHIP RULES OFTEN CONSIDERED INAPPROPRIATE

1. Partners are to share equally in both income and capital profits of the business and to contribute equally to losses.
2. Each partner is to be indemnified in respect of payments and liabilities incurred in the ordinary course of business or in anything necessarily done for the preservation of the firm's property.
3. Partners are to receive interest at 5% per annum on advances to the partnership beyond the amount of the capital they have agreed to subscribe.
4. There is to be no interest on capital contributions.
5. No partner is to receive remuneration apart from his share of partnership profits (e.g. no salaries).
6. Every partner may take part in the management of the partnership.
7. Unanimity is required for the introduction of a new partner or a change in the nature of the business.
8. Matters other than those referred to at 7. are to be decided by majority vote.
9. Every partner may inspect and copy the accounts which are to be kept at the principal place of business.
10. A majority of partners cannot expel a partner unless a power to do so has been conferred by express agreement (i.e. unanimity is required – s25).
11. If no fixed term has been agreed, then any partner may end the partnership by giving notice to all the other partners (and this can even be oral notice unless the partnership has an agreement in the form of a deed – s26).
12. The partnership is to be dissolved on (ss 32, 33):
    (a) the expiration of a fixed term;
    (b) the completion of a single adventure or undertaking, if the partnership was formed for that purpose;
    (c) the giving of notice or the end of a period of notice if the partnership was for an undefined term;
    (d) the death or bankruptcy of a partner; and
    (e) at the option of the partners, on a partner suffering his share to be charged with his separate debt.
13. On dissolution every partner is entitled to have the property of the partnership applied in the payment of debts and liabilities and the surplus assets applied to pay what is due to the partners (s 38).
14. In the case of a delayed settlement on death or cessation as a partner, a partner in the absence of any agreement to the contrary is entitled at his option to the share of profits attributable to the use of his share of partnership assets or interest at 5% on his share (s 42).

NB The first nine rules are set out in Section 24 Partnership Act 1890 and are expressed to be "subject to any agreement, express or implied between the partners"

Points to Watch

As a matter of style a partnership agreement should ideally provide a complete statement of the respective rights and obligations, even if this means repeating provisions implied by the Partnership Act. The clients are likely to refer to the document without the help of their solicitor in the future and will expect the contents to reflect the complete code of rules applicable to them.

Section 19 provides that "The mutual rights and duties of partners, whether ascertained by agreement or defined by this Act, may be varied by consent of all the partners, and such consent may be either express or inferred from a course of dealing".

It should be noted that this section not only provides a general ability to displace the statutory rules but also provides an ongoing amendment mechanism, which need not be evidenced in writing, to oust both the statutory provisions and any partnership agreement. Care must therefore be taken when advising clients in an existing partnership to establish, *inter alia,* whether the agreement set down in the formal partnership agreement has in fact been amended by course of conduct.

PARTNERSHIP INSTRUCTION CHECKLIST

1. Business name or names of all partners?
2. Actual date of commencement/intended date.
3. Proposed duration;
   fixed term?
   notice provision?
4. Place(s) of business.
5. Partnership property;
   what is it to comprise?
   how will it be held?
6. What will the partners contribute to the partnership?
   if unequal contributions, will interest be paid on capital and at what rate?
7. In what proportion will profits and losses be shared?
   is there to be a separate ratio for income/capital profits?
   are any salaries to be paid to partners before profits are shared out?
   how are fees from outside sources to be dealt with?
8. Drawings;
   maximum limits?
   interest on amounts overdrawn?
9. Who are the firm's bankers to be?
   who will sign cheques?
   will specified sums require more than one signature?
10. To what date will accounts be drawn up?
    on what basis?
11. Will majority decisions govern all ordinary matters?
    will there be a separate management committee?
12. Will a partner be able to assign or bequeath his share in the partnership?
    will a partner be able to nominate a new partner?
13. What will the duties of each partner be?
14. Holiday entitlement and notice.
15. Will each partner be required to devote the whole of his time and attention to partnership business?
    will partners be entitled to be concerned directly or interested in another business with or without consent of fellow partners?
    provisions restricting competition on leaving the firm?
16. Prohibition on individual partners charging their interest in the firm?
17. New partners:
    when and how can they be admitted?
18. Provision for retirement:
    on notice?
    compulsory at certain age?

19. Provision for expulsion:
    in what circumstances?
    by majority?
20. Payment of partnership share on death/retirement/expulsion:
    in instalments?
    option to dissolve or purchase?
21. Requirements concerning pension provision/insurance etc.
22. Handling disputes:
    - arbitration clause?

Partnership Name

As in the case of the formation of a company, the choice of a partnership name will often be a subject close to the partners' hearts. They may wish simply to use a combination of their own surnames (as is particularly common when dealing with professional partnerships). On the other hand, especially in the case of a trading partnership, they may wish to use an entirely separate business name. Although there is no longer a register of business names, there are nevertheless a number of constraints which must be observed, namely:

1. The last word in the name must not be "Limited" or its Welsh equivalent (s 34 CA), but the use of "& Co." is however allowed since this has no precise legal meaning;
2. Unless the name comprises merely the surnames of all partners (and the corporate names of any corporate partners) without an addition other than a permitted addition (basically surnames or initials and an indication that the business is carried on in succession to a former owner) then it constitutes a "business name" under the Business Names Act 1985, and as such:
    a) unless the Secretary of State gives written approval, the name must not convey the impression that the business is connected with Her Majesty's Government or with any local authority;
    b) unless either the Secretary of State or the person specified by him gives approval, it must not include any word or expression specified in the Company and Business Names Regulations 1981 (see p9 ante).

Registration for VAT Purposes

For VAT purposes a partnership is required to register if its taxable supplies in the last 12 months exceeded £47,000 or if there are reasonable grounds for believing that the value of its taxable supplies during the ensuing 30 days will exceed that figure. A new partnership is unlikely to meet these figures but still has the option to register voluntarily if it is making taxable supplies beneath that figure. Section 45 Value Added Tax Act 1994 provides that registration may be in the firm name, effectively therefore treating the partnership for VAT purposes as a single taxable person. It follows that the partnership will be deemed to continue for VAT purposes despite the appointment of new partners or the retirement of existing ones.

Financial Structure

Careful consideration will have to be given to the capital requirements of the business and decisions taken as to the contribution which each partner is to make. If contributions are to be unequal, provision will need to be made to compensate for the imbalance (e.g. by the use of interest on capital, partnership salary or perhaps even a lesser work commitment).

Contributions may be made both in cash and kind, the latter being particularly appropriate where assets currently held by an individual partner are required for the partnership business to function. The partnership itself, not being a separate legal person, cannot be the legal owner of such assets. Instead it is usual for one or more of the partners to hold them on trust for the partnership and for the status of such assets to be expressly declared in the partnership agreement, hence avoiding disputes in the future as to the precise nature of partnership property.

A loan obtained to fund a contribution should fall within the ambit of Section 362 Income and Corporation Taxes Act 1988 and constitute a "qualifying loan" for income tax purposes. Any interest paid should therefore be deductible as a charge on income from the income of the individual in question.

CHAPTER 9

Day to Day Running

CHAPTER 9

Day to Day Running

Partners' duties

Those clients entering the partnership relationship for the first time are unlikely to appreciate the impact of the general duty of good faith which fellow partners owe to each other. Like directors of a company, partners themselves are placed in a fiduciary position and as such must behave towards each other with utmost fairness. The duty is said to be overriding in the sense that it will apply notwithstanding the provisions of any partnership agreement.

In order to impress upon clients the importance of this duty, it is suggested that it should actually be reiterated in the written partnership agreement.

Although the general duty is not expressed in the Partnership Act, three particular aspects of the duty are specified, namely:

Section 28 Partnership Act 1890

"Partners are bound to render true accounts and full information of all things affecting the partnership to any partner or his legal representatives"

If for any reason information is withheld from a partner, then he will have the option of settling aside any resulting agreement.

Section 29 Partnership Act 1890

"Every partner must account to the firm for any benefit derived by him without the consent of the firm from any transaction concerning the partnership or from any use by him of the partnership property, name or business connection".

This section applies even if:

- the benefit was made innocently
- the firm itself could not have denied that particular benefit or would not have wished to do so.

Any benefit caught by Section 29 will be brought into partnership profits and shared out between all the partners in accordance with the profit sharing arrangement.

Practical Tip

Advice to partner who anticipates application of Section 29.

- disclose all material facts to fellow partners
- obtain fellow partners' agreement in writing that he should proceed on a personal basis.

Section 30 Partnership Act 1890

"If a partner, without the consent of the other partners, carries on any business of the same nature as and competing with that of the firm, he must account for and pay over to the firm all profits made by him in that business".

This only covers businesses of the same nature which actually compete with the partnership business. It is therefore common to extend the requirement by agreement to include businesses which are not of the same nature and even non-competing businesses.

Business Name Formalities

If a business name has been adopted, the partnership will be required to meet certain disclosure requirements, namely:

(a) A statement must appear on all business letters, invoices, orders, receipts and demands for payment of debts of:
   (i) the names of all partners;
   (ii) a UK address for each partner where service of documents relating to the business would be effective.

(b) A notice containing the names and addresses referred to above must be displayed in a prominent position at any premises where the business is carried on and to which customers or suppliers have access.

(c) These details must also be supplied immediately in writing on request to persons with whom the partnership deals in the course of business.

Failure to comply with these rules constitutes a criminal offence and should a third party be able to show that he has been unable to pursue a claim against the business arising out of a contract because of the failure or he has suffered a financial loss in connection with a contract because of such a breach, then an action against him for breach of contract will be dismissed.

Entering Into Contracts

It is relatively common for a single partner to enter into contracts on behalf of the partnership and such a contract will obviously bind the partnership if the partner in question is actually authorised to enter into such contracts. It may be however that he has not specifically been authorised to enter into such contracts in which case the partnership will only be bound if either:

(a) it can be said that the power to enter into such contracts must be implied into the actual authority which he has been given; or

(b) he has ostensible usual authority to do so.

Rather than leave the question of usual authority to general common law principles, the Partnership Act expresses the principles in statutory form in Section 5 which effectively provides that if the partner is doing an act for the carrying on in the usual way business of the kind carried on by the firm the partnership will be bound unless:

(a) he in fact has no authority to act for the firm in the particular manner; and

(b) the person with whom he is dealing either knows he has no authority or does not know or believe him to be a partner (see p114 post).

Accounts

The accounts of a partnership, unlike those of a limited company, are a private document and as such are not required to comply with a detailed statutory form. Nevertheless detailed accounts will be required both for commercial and taxation purposes. In drawing up these accounts a large number of partnerships will decide not to value the "goodwill" of the partnership. Goodwill is a difficult concept to define. In accountant's terms it is the additional sum which a prospective purchaser of a business is prepared to pay for a business in excess of its net assets. In lawyers' terms it has been said to be "the whole advantage whatever it may be, of the reputation and connection of the firm" (*Lord Macnaghten Trego* v *Hunt* [1896] AC 26). Failure to value this asset, however elusive, may lead to capital gain tax problems.

Taxation of partnerships

Any partnership set up after 6 April 1994 is subject to a new income tax regime, instigated as part of simplified self assessment, which removes many of the complexities previously associated with partnership income taxation. This regime will also apply to all existing partnerships in full from the tax year 1997–8 at the latest. It is therefore proposed to deal only with the new regime.

Partners setting up a new partnership will be relieved to discover that they are, amongst other things, no longer jointly and severally liable for income tax on their partner's partnership income. The new regime is at least theoretically simple: partners are taxed as individuals on a current year basis on their individual shares of the partnership profit determined by reference to their actual profit shares in the accounting periods during which the profits arose.

1. Complications

1. The current year basis means that in a tax year the profits of the accounting period ending in that year are assessed (i.e. it is not an actual tax year basis). For example:

   A partnership makes up its accounts to 31 December in each year.

Accounting Period	January 1997	January 1998	January 1999
Tax Year	April 1997	April 1998	April 1999

   In tax year 1998–9 the profits of accounting period 1 January 1998–31 December 1998 will be charged (i.e. the profits of the accounting period ending in the tax year).
2. The partnership itself is technically treated as an individual and therefore is obliged to submit a tax return.
3. Each partner is treated as notionally carrying on his share of the partnership business and therefore when he joins the partnership a set of special rules concerning commencement of a business apply and when he leaves another special set re termination of a business come into play.
   These are basically:
   (a) In the tax year a partner joins the partnership his assessment will be based on his actual partnership profits for that year, in the second tax year the assessment will be based on his share of the profits for the accounting period ending in that year (or if that period is of less than 12 months, the 12 month period beginning on the date he became a partner).
   (b) In the tax year that he leaves the partnership, the period of profits taken will

be the period that begins immediately after the end of the previous period charged to tax and ends on discontinuance.

If as result of these rules an amount of profits is included in his tax computation for two successive years, a form of relief known as "overlap relief" will be given.

The partnership trading profits will fall under Schedule D, Case 1 and will therefore be ascertained by calculating chargeable receipts less deductible expenses. It should be noted that partners' salaries and interest paid on capital contributions do not constitute deductible expenses for these purposes.

The capital gains tax position of partnerships continues to be complex. The Revenue in trying to determine capital gains tax liability have continually had to grapple with the technical problem that a partnership is not a separate legal entity. Their solutions to this problem and their analysis of how a CGT regime designed to apply to single legal entities is to be applied to partnerships is set out in SP D12 and in cases of doubt there is still no real substitute for referring to its detailed wording.

The basic principle is straightforward. Each partner is treated as owning a fractional share in each of the partnership chargeable assets. The amount of this share is determined by referring to the share in which partners have agreed to allocate asset surpluses (known as the "asset surplus sharing ratio" or "assr"). If partners have not set out a separate ratio for sharing these capital profits, the normal profit sharing ratio will apply.

On the disposal of a partnership asset each partner will therefore be treated as having disposed of the appropriate share of the asset in return for the appropriate share of the consideration, and his liability will be calculated by deducting the appropriate share of the base cost (calculated by taking his asset at the time of acquisition) as increased by the indexation allowance. Although the Revenue will be able to substitute market value for actual consideration if the transaction is not a bargain at arms length and will automatically do so in the case of a transaction between connected persons, it should be noted that Section 286(4) TCGA 1992 provides that: "Except in relation to acquisition or disposals of partnership assets pursuant to bona fide commercial arrangements, a person is connected with any person with whom he is in partnership, and with the husband or wife or a relative of any individual with whom he is in partnership", i.e. so long as parties are acting bona fide and commercially *inter se* they will not be treated as connected because of their partnership.

2. CGT Implications on Disposal of an Asset to a Third Party

The following example illustrates the CGT treatment of the disposal of an asset to a third party.

A, B & C share profits, both income and capital, equally.

They purchased an asset in 1993, when they also shared profits equally, for £30,000.

They are now disposing of it to a third party for £60,000.

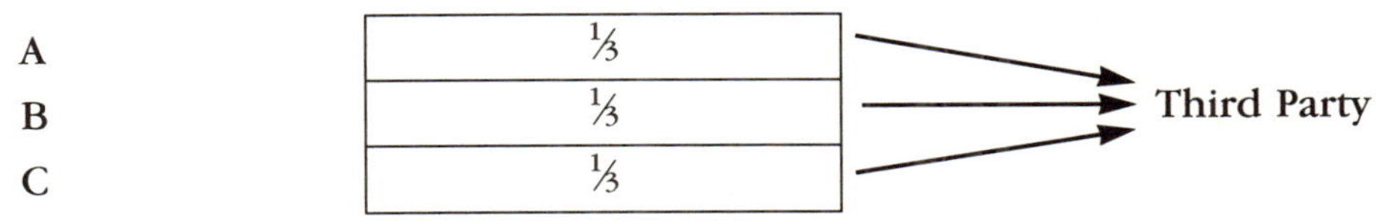

Each will be treated as disposing of their ⅓ share for £20,000 (i.e. ⅓ of £60,000) and will have an acquisition cost of £10,000 (i.e. ⅓ of £30,000). *Prima facie* gain of each (ignoring indexation) is therefore £10,000.

CHAPTER 10

The Developmental Phase

CHAPTER 10

The Developmental Phase

The time may come when a successful partnership wishes to expand its business. By nature partnerships are usually relatively small enterprises or are professional firms. If the partners wish to develop the business it may be that the best commercial option is to consider incorporation. Particularly if they are hoping to encourage outsiders to invest in the business, a partnership may not be regarded as the most attractive proposition. Many potential investors will ideally be looking for an investment where they have the benefits of a share in profits and of limited liability if the business becomes insolvent (see p2 ante). It is possible to form a partnership where some of the partners have limited liability under the Limited Partnerships Act 1907 however this is not as practical a solution as incorporation. Should, however, incorporation not be an option, the following should be considered.

Raising New Capital

The usual ways to raise new capital are through the introduction of a new partner or by means of a loan. The relative characteristics of each course of action are considered below:

1. Taking on a New Partner

1. Long term capital contribution in the sense that it remains in the partnership until the partner leaves.
2. Requirement of profit share will undermine profits of existing partners unless and until a corresponding rise in profits occurs.
3. Participation in management means a shift in the power base.
4. Ability to bind the partnership exposes existing partners to risk.
5. Payment of profit share is not a deductible expense.

2. Borrowing Money

1. Fixed term contribution.
2. Fixed interest payments whether or not profits arise.
3. Paid in priority to partners on insolvency of partnership.
4. No rights to participate in management.
5. No ability to bind partners vis-à-vis outsiders.
6. Payment of interest should constitute a deductible expense.

Introduction of New Partner

A new partner can only be introduced if all the existing partners consent (s 24(7) Partnership Act 1890). This is subject to contrary agreement and it may be that a particular partner with seniority will have been given the power to introduce a new partner in the partnership agreement. The close working relationship and need for trust within a partnership, exemplified by the duty of good faith and the ability of partners to make each other liable for outside debts, means that great care must be taken in assessing the suitability of any potential new partner. It is suggested that as a bare minimum the existing partners should consider the following:

CHECKLIST FOR ASSESSING SUITABILITY OF NEW PARTNER

1. What is he able to contribute in terms of capital?
2. What does he anticipate in the way of profit share?
   (*Note:* salaries and interest on capital are taken out before dividing the balance in the profit sharing ratio).
3. What does he require from the partnership in terms of personal cash flow, drawings etc?
4. What can he contribute to the partnership in terms of work/contacts etc?
5. Can he get on with the existing partners on a personal level?

There are no internal formalities to consider with such an introduction beyond anything specified in the agreement although negotiations will have to be completed to establish, *inter alia,* how much capital is to be injected, the appropriate profit shares and management powers of the partners. It may be that the introduction of a new partner would upset the power structure: for example, if there were originally two partners and it is now proposed that there should be three this may have an adverse affect in that one partner may have lost his effective veto on day to day decisions. The new partner may be willing to be a "sleeping partner" and wish to take no active role in the firm's management. This can however be precarious as such a partner will have no power over how the firm is run but will remain liable for its debts without limit.

The new partner's capital contribution will be shown as such in the accounts and he will *prima facie* become entitled to his agreed share in profits for the proportion of the accounting year in which he joins. The contribution of capital itself has no immediate tax consequences, however the acquisition of a right to share in asset surpluses (usually by allocation of his share in profits) will inevitably mean that a disposal of part of the share of an existing partner/partners will be taking place and as such a disposal of a chargeable asset for capital gains tax purposes will occur. However, no charge to capital gains tax will arise unless either:

(a) There has been a revaluation of the capital assets of the partnership;
(b) A payment is made for the share outside the accounts e.g. a premium for goodwill which has not been valued in the accounts is paid by the incoming partner to the existing partners;
(c) The arrangement is of a non-commercial nature (i.e. the persons involved are connected in some way other than as partners, or the deal is otherwise non-commercial).

The new partner will be subject to the opening year rules, see p104 ante, on his share of income profits, however, the other partners will be unaffected by his joining and their income tax liability will continue on a current year basis.

Points to Watch

Another way to increase the firm's capital albeit on a small scale is to limit the drawings of the partners in the partnership agreement. A clause in the agreement could direct that the undrawn profits each year are added to the partner's capital.

Loan Capital

If no suitable new partner can be found and the existing partners do not wish to contribute further capital, the firm's only viable option to raise money may be to borrow. The loan may come from institutional lenders, from the partners themselves or contacts. The characteristics of loan capital have already been considered when looking at companies raising finance. The same basic points apply to partnership (see p46 ante) although there is much less scope to borrow money than with companies. If the business itself is on a small scale, few lenders will be willing to lend large sums of money without security and although a partnership may give a fixed charge as security, it is incapable of creating a floating charge. This may effectively limit the amount of loan capital it can attract, since if it is already undercapitalised there may be few fixed assets capable of charging. If the firm's major asset is its stock in trade for example this asset cannot be used in the business and be subject to a fixed charge. In this situation incorporation should be considered, as the resultant company could execute a floating charge.

Should a suitable lender be found, interest payments on the loan will constitute a deductible expense in calculating the partnership's Schedule D, Case I profits, provided, for example, they can be said to be wholly and exclusively incurred for the purposes of the trade and do not offend against the statutory provisions which limit deductibility (s 74 CTA 1988 etc).

Formalities

The power to borrow can be limited under the partnership agreement. It may be that the power to borrow and give security can only be exercised by the partners unanimously. Subject to express provisions in the partnership agreement however no formalities will be required other than proper execution of the documents and if, there is a fixed charge over land, registration of that charge at HM Land Registry or Land Charges Department as appropriate.

Points to Consider

- Should the partnership incorporate?
- Is there a proper procedure in place for the introduction of a new partner?
- Is is possible to limit drawings and direct undrawn profits to be added to capital?
- Loan capital – secured or unsecured? Fixed charge possible but not floating charge.
- Existing partner may borrow money to lend to the firm.

CHAPTER 11

Dealing with Disputes

CHAPTER 11

Dealing with Disputes

Having set up a partnership and perhaps advised on its future development, the solicitor may find that he is not consulted again until some form of dispute arises. He may also be consulted by new partnership clients on the occurrence of a dispute. Disputes fall into two categories, those which may involve a problem between the partners themselves and those which concern the partnership's liability to outsiders.

Disputes Between the Partners

In considering disputes between the partners it will always be necessary to establish first how their relationship is regulated. If the solicitor set up the partnership himself he can refer to the partnership agreement, although he must take care to establish whether this has been varied by further agreement or by a course of dealing (s 19 PA – see p98 ante). However, if dealing with a new client he may find that the partnership has no formal partnership agreement and will therefore probably be a partnership at will and governed by the implied terms of the Partnership Act 1890. This will mean, *inter alia,* that the duty of good faith found in Sections 28–30 applies and that all the rules implied by Section 24 govern the internal workings of the partnership (see p97 ante) will be applicable unless excluded pursuant to Section 19. If the partnership is a partnership at will and the problem cannot be resolved a partner will be able to dissolve the partnership by giving notice of dissolution to the other partners (ss 26 and 32).

If a partnership agreement exists the following checklist should be followed:

CHECKLIST FOR PARTNERSHIP DISPUTES

1. Does the partnership agreement specifically provide a solution to the dispute in question?
2. Has the relevant provision in the partnership agreement been varied by subsequent agreement or course of dealings?
3. If there is no such provision can the dispute be resolved by negotiating a compromise?
4. If such resolution is not possible or its terms are uncertain, is there an arbitration clause providing for a third party arbitration?

Points to Watch

A properly drafted partnership agreement will usually contain an arbitration clause. Such a clause cannot oust the court's jurisdiction to deal with a dispute altogether but if an action is commenced despite the clause the court will usually stay proceedings pending the outcome of the arbitration.

There is no equivalent in a partnership to company law's unfairly prejudicial conduct based petition (s 459 Companies Act 1985). Any internal dispute is governed by the Act or the partnership agreement. Although a partner may petition the court to dissolve the partnership under Section 35 (e.g. s 35(f) on the just and equitable ground equivalent to s 122 (i)(g) Insolvency Act 1986 for companies) this is extremely rare in practice as he can either dissolve the partnership by notice (if partnership at will) or force the other partners to buy him out or in default agree to a dissolution (matters dealt with in a partnership deed).

Disputes over whether property is partnership property and the carrying on of another business by a partner are two of the most frequent causes of inter-party friction. The following checklists should be used when addressing these two problems.

Disputes over Partnership Property

1. Look for express agreement (e.g. statement in a transfer of the property in question or in the partnership agreement).
2. Look for implied agreement (e.g. asset is shown as partnership asset in the partnership accounts).
3. Rely on the following statutory presumptions if applicable:
   (a) property bought with partnership money is deemed to have been bought on account of the firm (s 21); and
   (b) property brought into the partnership stock or acquired on account of the firm or for the purposes of the firm in the course of the partnership business is deemed to be partnership property (s 20).

Point to Watch
Both Sections 20 and 21 are subject to contrary intention.

4. Failing 1–3, a court may be prepared to infer, for example, from a course of dealing that property is partnership property, however they will only be prepared to do so if it is necessary to give business efficacy to an agreement.

Point to Watch
The fact that the property was originally co-owned by partners does not of itself convert it into partnership property.

Partner Carrying on Another Business Without Consent

1. Is the business of the same nature and competing with the partnership business? If so claim all profits made.
2. If the business does not fall within Section 30 is he nevertheless using partnership profit or business connection or does the transaction otherwise concern the partnership? If so claim profits under Section 29.
3. Do his activities breach such terms of the partnership agreement as the obligation to devote whole time to the business of the partnership or the obligation not to carry on any other business? If these or any other terms are breached, claim damages/injunction.

Disputes Between Partners and Third Parties

1. Contractual

Every partner is liable without limit for partnership debts incurred while he is a partner, although he may have a right of contribution from the other partners (s 9). New partners are only liable for debts incurred after they join the firm. Unless there is a novation of pre-existing contracts which will normally need to be express but may also be inferred from conduct (e.g. paying old debts) the new partner will not be liable on those old debts.

All the partners and the firm are bound when someone (whether or not a partner) acts with actual authority (s 6). Actual authority may either be express, that is authority specifically agreed upon by the partners, or implied from a course of dealings between the partners. The partnership agreement may specify the role of the partners and their particular powers. A third party can rely on an action taken by anyone who is acting within his actual authority and can enforce such rights against the firm.

A third party is also entitled to assume that a partner has authority to bind the firm in certain circumstances where the partner is deemed to have ostensible/usual authority. This principle is laid down in Section 5:

> *"Every partner is an agent of the firm and his other partners for the purpose of the business of the partnership; and the acts of every partner who does any act for carrying on in the usual way business of the kind carried on by the firm of which he is a member bind the firm and his partners, unless the partner so acting has in fact no authority to act for the firm in the particular matter, and the person with whom he is dealing knows that he has no authority or does not know or believe him to be a partner."*

The wording of the section is slightly tortuous, but if considered in stages its meaning becomes clear. Firstly, the partner can only bind the firm "for the purposes of the business of the partnership". The partner will not therefore bind the firm by all his actions. Only his actions which are consistent with the type of business carried on by the firm will come within the section. In deciding what the firm's business is, it is important not only to consider what is stated in the partnership agreement but also what business appears to be carried on to the outside world.

Similarly, the firm will only be bound if the partner's act can be considered as "carrying on in the usual way the business of the firm" conventionally referred to as "usual authority". The firm will therefore not be liable for an act which, even though carried out for the purposes of the business, is of an unusual type. One example might be a partner allowing a firm's debtor to pay his debt in kind rather than money.

The final point is that the firm is not bound where the partner in question has no actual authority and the third party either knows this or does not know or believe the person he is dealing with to be a partner. Obviously in such circumstances the third party cannot claim that he believed he was entering a transaction with the partnership.

If the partnership is not liable on a contract under either Sections 5 or 6, the partner himself will be liable to the third party for breach of warranty of authority.

2. Tortious Liability

The partnership as whole will be liable for any loss or injury caused to a non-partner by the wrongful act or omission of any partner acting in the ordinary course of the business of the partnership (s 10).

USUAL AUTHORITY			
	Always in usual authority		*Never in usual authority*
i)	Buying and selling goods in relation to firm's business.	i)	executing deed on behalf of the firm.
ii)	engaging or dismissing employees.	ii)	giving a guarantee in the firm's name (unless this is customary in the trade).
iii)	giving a receipt in respect of payment of debts owed to the firm. **and in a trading partnership**	iii)	accepting property in lieu of money owed to the firm.
iv)	borrowing money on behalf of the firm.	iv)	submitting any dispute between the parties to arbitration.
v)	dealing in any way in negotiable instruments in the name of the firm.		
vi)	pledging any goods belonging to the firm.		
vii)	creating an equitable mortgage by deposit of title deeds to property owned by the firm.		

Suing or Being Sued

Although a partnership has no separate legal identity the partners may sue or be sued in the firm's name (RSC Ord 81). If the firm is being sued, the writ may be served on any partner, any person having control or management of the business at the principal place of business, or by post to the principal place of business.

A third party who has a judgment against a partner in his personal capacity may enforce the judgment against that partner's partnership share by way of charging order.

Points to Consider

- Is the dispute internal between the partners or does it involve the partnership's potential liability to outsiders?
- Is there a formal agreement governing partners' relationship *inter se* or does the Partnership Act 1890 apply?
- A partnership agreement may contain the solution or require the partners to go to arbitration. Partners may agree to go to arbitration in any event.
- Partners have unlimited liability for the firm's debts incurred whilst they are partners.
- Partners who have actual authority will bind the firm in dealings with third parties.
- The firm will also be bound if a partner acts with usual ostensible authority under Section 5.

CHAPTER 12

Leaving the Partnership

CHAPTER 12

Leaving the Partnership

Leaving the Partnership

There are various events which give rise to the departure of a partner from the firm. The partner may wish to retire or pursue other business interests, the other partners may wish to expel him or indeed he may die. A solicitor who is asked to advise clients in these circumstances needs to have a clear understanding of the principles contained in the Partnership Act and the ways in which these can be varied by a partnership agreement. These and other matters are dealt with in Chapter 12.

Dissolution of the Partnership

The terms of the Partnership Act 1890 provide that dissolution will occur in certain circumstances subject to an agreement to the contrary. Under the Act dissolution can occur in circumstances where it may be the last thing the partners want, or at the whim of one particular partner against the will of the majority. Dissolution leads to the partnership ceasing and its assets being realised. The effect is therefore similar to a company being wound up. As dissolution is such an extreme measure, it is always advisable to provide expressly in the partnership agreement that dissolution is not to occur automatically on the occurrence of the circumstances specified in the Act.

1. Grounds for Dissolution

The partnership agreement may expressly exclude the statutory grounds for dissolution and specify particular occurrences which will cause dissolution. The agreement should also provide for the manner in which the partnership will be dissolved in terms of how the assets will be distributed (e.g. which partner if any is to be entitled to use the name of the firm after dissolution).

It is usual to provide that the partnership will not terminate on the departure of a partner if at least two of the remaining partners wish the firm to continue. Subject to such agreements to the contrary the Act provides for dissolution in the following circumstances:

(a) Any partner may dissolve the partnership by giving notice to the other partners (s 26 and s 32 (c)). If the partnership was originally constituted by deed the notice must be in writing signed by the partner giving it. The partnership is dissolved as from the date mentioned in the notice as the date of dissolution, or, if no date is mentioned, as from the date of the communication of the notice to all the partners. This potential power of immediate dissolution could lead to serious practical problems for the firm and therefore such power to dissolve may be excluded or made subject to a minimum notice period in the partnership agreement.

(b) Section 32 (a) and (b) provide for dissolution if the partnership was entered for a fixed term which has expired or if entered into for a single adventure or undertaking which has terminated. If the partnership continues after this time, Section 27 provides that the partnership becomes a partnership at will dissolvable by notice, on the same terms which were applicable before the occurrence of the event under Section 32 (a) or (b).

(c) Section 33 provides for automatic dissolution on the death or bankruptcy of any partner. It also gives the other partners an option to dissolve the partnership if a partner suffers his partnership share to be charged for his own personal debts. The partnership agreement will usually exclude this section and often will treat death of a partner as leading to the same consequences as retirement and bankruptcy as leading to the same consequences as expulsion.

Point to Watch
If a creditor succeeds in obtaining a charging order over a partner's share this gives the other partners an option to dissolve. They may decide to do so or they may pay the debt and recover the amount paid out of the partner's share or from the partner personally if the share is insufficient (s 23).

In the three situations above the partnership will be dissolved unless the partnership agreement expresses a contrary intent. The Act also provides for dissolution in other ways which cannot be excluded by agreement. Section 34 provides for automatic dissolution on the happening of any event which makes it unlawful for the business of the firm to be carried on or for the members of the firm to carry it on in partnership. Therefore if the partnership is formed for a purpose which was initially lawful but due to a change in the law becomes unlawful the partnership is dissolved.

It is also possible for a partner to apply to the court for dissolution on proof of one of the statutory grounds. This course of conduct is unusual, since if the partnership is a partnership at will it can be dissolved by notice. If there is a formal partnership agreement it will usually allow a disgruntled partner to retire and realise his share, or take his grievance to arbitration. Application to the court will therefore usually be regarded as a needless expense. Such an application is however possible under Section 35 Partnership Act 1890 on the following grounds:

(i) permanent incapability of a partner performing his part of the partnership agreement.
(ii) conduct of a partner calculated to be prejudicial to the carrying on of the business.
(iii) a partner wilfully or persistently commits breaches of the partnership agreement.
(iv) the business of the partnership can only be carried on at a loss.
(v) it is just and equitable that the partnership be dissolved.

In addition to the above the court has power under the Mental Health Act 1983 to dissolve the partnership if a partner becomes a mental patient.

2. Realisation of Partnership Assets

Once it is established that the partnership is to be dissolved the assets and affairs of the firm must be wound up. The assets will be realised and the firm's debts and liabilities must be paid before the surplus is distributed amongst the partners. Section 38 states that after the dissolution the authority of each partner to bind the firm continues in so far as may be necessary to wind up the affairs of the partnership and to complete any transaction outstanding at the time of the dissolution but not otherwise. The winding up of the partnership assets may be achieved by the partners agreeing to sell off the assets piecemeal or by their agreeing to sell the business as a going concern.

Section 39 allows each partner to insist that the firm's assets are applied in payment of the firm's debts and liabilities and to have the surplus distributed amongst the partners in the correct proportion. If there is a dispute in relation to this distribution any partner may apply to the court to wind up the firm's assets. The court will usually appoint a receiver or receiver and manager to realise and distribute the assets.

3. Distribution of Partnership Assets

Section 44 contains the rules for settling accounts between the partners on a distribution. It is subject to an agreement to the contrary in the partnership agreement. These rules provide that the assets shall be applied in the following order:

1. in paying the debts and liabilities of the firm;
2. in repaying advances made by a partner to the firm as distinguished from his capital contribution;
3. in repaying amounts standing to the credit of partners' capital account;
4. the residue is divided between the partners in accordance with the profit sharing ratio.

If the firm has made losses including losses and deficiencies of capital, those losses are to be paid for in the following order:

- out of profits
- out of capital
- by the partners in proportion to the profit sharing ratio.

> **Point to Watch**
> If the assets are sufficient to pay the firm's outside creditors but insufficient to repay the partners' capital, the firm is deemed to have made a loss to which the partners are liable to contribute in their profit sharing ratio, unless otherwise agreed.

It is, however, common for the partnership agreement to provide for contributions to capital losses to be paid for in a ratio different to the normal profit sharing ratio especially where the partners have markedly different capital contributions.

Retirement, Expulsion, Death or Bankruptcy

Under the Partnership Act 1890 the effect of retirement, death or bankruptcy of a partner is to dissolve the partnership. There is no power under the Act to expel a partner for misconduct. Again dissolution is the only option. It is therefore essential for a partnership agreement to deal expressly with these issues. It is common to include a clause stating that a partner ceases to be a partner in any of these four situations but that if there are at least two remaining partners that the partnership shall not determine as regards the continuing partners. For instance, if a partner wishes to leave, there should be a specific clause dealing with retirement requiring that partner to give a specific notice period (e.g. three or six months). Once the notice period elapses he ceases to be a partner but the partnership continues without him.

Expulsion Clause

It will often be the case that the majority of partners will not wish to dissolve the partnership should a dispute arise but will wish to expel a partner. There is no implied power to expel a partner under Section 25 of the Act, and therefore it is common to include an expulsion clause within the partnership agreement.

If such a clause is included it will normally contain a list of specific activities which, if engaged in will make a partner liable for expulsion. Such behaviour as serious or persistent breaches of the agreement or being absent from the business for a particular number of days in a period of 12 months may trigger the expulsion. The clause will usually go on to state that if guilty of such conduct the partner may be expelled by written notice from the other partners with immediate effect.

Key Elements of an Expulsion Clause

The main points to be covered in an expulsion clause and the actions to be taken in the event of an expulsion, are as follows:

1. Define events of expulsion, avoiding such subjective criteria as "flagrant" breach or "unreasonable" unless such terms are defined in relation to the judgment of a person (e.g. "in the opinion of ....").
2. Provide for notice procedure, for example in writing with immediate effect.
3. Exclude consequential dissolution.
4. Deal with how expelled partner is to receive his share of assets and profits.
5. Provide for restrictions on his conduct post-expulsion (e.g. a non-solicitation restrictive covenant) but beware doctrine of restraint of trade.
6. Provide for notification of existing clients, customers etc.

> ***Point to watch***
> A power to expel is still subject to the duty of good faith – it must be used for the benefit of the firm and not for the personal gain of the remaining partners.

Option to Purchase Partnership Share

If someone ceases to be a partner there should be express provision in the partnership agreement entitling the other partners to purchase his share and continue the business. It may state that if any of the remaining partners do not wish to purchase the share the partnership shall be dissolved.

The partnership agreement may allow for the provision of a pension for the outgoing partner or his dependants. It must deal with how the outgoing partner's share is to be valued and paid for. It may be financially impossible for the other partners to raise at short notice enough funds to buy out the share in one lump sum. The agreement should provide a formula for ascertaining the value of the partner's share including the value of his portion of the business (including goodwill), the debts and liabilities of the firm, and any undrawn balances of profits. It may be appropriate for the value to be certified by the partnership accountant.

In order to deal with the problem of raising funds it is usual to allow for the purchase price to be paid by instalments, for example four 6-monthly instalments of equal value with interest on the instalments for the time being remaining unpaid. Insurance cover in the case of death of a partner should also be considered.

Liability of Outgoing Partner

1. Liabilities Incurred Prior to Leaving

Section 9 Partnership Act 1890 provides that a partner is liable without limit for debts incurred by the partnership while he is a partner. This is subject to a right of contribution from the other partners. Also relevant to a retiring partner is Section 17(2) which states that a partner who retires does not thereby cease to be liable for partnership debts or obligations incurred before his retirement. A partner who retires is therefore still liable for the firm's debts incurred whilst he was a partner. Section 17(3) may provide some protection for him in relation to such debts as it allows for his discharge from such liabilities if an agreement to such effect is entered into expressly or by conduct between the remaining partners and the creditors. Such novation is unlikely in practice.

In order to protect himself from continuing liability on debts owed prior to his retirement a partner should try to ensure that all such debts are paid prior to his leaving. The practicalities of the situation may not permit this, in which case he should obtain an indemnity from the remaining partners that if he should become liable to pay such debts they will compensate him on a £ for £ basis.

2. Liabilities Incurred After Leaving

In theory a partner is only liable for debts incurred whilst he was a partner and therefore will not normally be liable for debts incurred after his departure. The outgoing partner must be aware of Sections 14 and 36 and take care to avoid potential liability for future debts under these two sections.

Section 14 deals with the situation where a person is being held out as a partner even if he is not one. It states that everyone who represents himself or who knowingly suffers himself to be represented as a partner, is liable as a partner to anyone who has on the faith of such a representation given credit to the firm. Care must therefore be taken to ensure that a partner who retires is not still held out as a partner. This would be a particular risk if the retiring partner continues to work for the firm in a consultancy capacity.

Section 14(2) provides that where the firm continues to use the old firm name after the death of a partner, the continued use of the name will not in itself make his estate liable for debts incurred after the partner's death.

In addition Section 36 provides as follows:

(i) *"Where a person deals with a firm after a change in its constitution he is entitled to treat all apparent members of the old firm as still being members of the firm until he has notice of the change."*

(ii) *"An advertisement in the London Gazette ... shall be notice as to persons who had not had dealings with the firm before the date of the dissolution or change so advertised."*

(iii) *"The estate of a partner who dies, or who becomes bankrupt, or of a partner who, not having been known to the person dealing with the firm to be a partner, retires from the firm, is not liable for partnership debts contracted after the date of the death, bankruptcy, or retirement respectively."*

The net effect is that the following notices are required:

Category of person	*Notice required*
Persons dealing with the firm who also dealt with it before his retirement.	Circulate with actual notice of retirement s 30(1).
Persons who have not dealt with the firm prior to his retirement but nevertheless knew him to be a partner.	Give constructive notice in *London Gazette* s 36(2).
Persons who have not dealt with the firm or did not know him to be a partner.	No notice required.

The combined effect of Sections 14 and 36 is that an outgoing partner or his representatives must ensure that certain formalities are dealt with in order to prevent potential liability for the future debts of the firm:

CHECKLIST

1. Actual notice to customers, creditors and those who have dealt with the firm in the past.
2. Notice in *London Gazette.*
3. Alteration of any nameplates or stationery bearing partner's name. Safer still, their destruction. This should help to avoid holding out under Section 14 and ensure compliance with the Business Names Act 1985.
4. Notice to Inland Revenue and H.M. Customs and Excise.
5. Notice to bank: alter bank mandate.
6. Notices as necessary for partnership assets (e.g. to insurance companies).
7. Transfer of partnership property to other partners.

Points to Consider

- As with much partnership law there are two possible scenarios. The partnership may have no formal agreement, in which case the provisions of the Partnership Act 1890 will apply. Alternatively, the partners will have executed a formal partnership deed excluding many of the Act's provisions.
- If the Act applies and the firm is a partnership at will, the retirement, death or bankruptcy of a partner will cause the dissolution of the partnership. Application to the court for dissolution will in normal circumstances be unnecessary.
- On dissolution the firm will be wound up and its assets distributed according to the statutory order. Any dispute in relation to this can be resolved by application to the court for the appointment of a receiver or receiver and manager to realise and distribute the assets.
- A properly drafted partnership agreement should expressly provide for a partnership to continue in business following the retirement, death or bankruptcy of a partner. It will usually also include a power to expel a partner in certain circumstances.
- The agreement should provide an option for the remaining partners to purchase the partnership share of the outgoing partners.
- The outgoing partner should take the necessary steps to protect himself from liability for partnership debts incurred after he leaves and as far as possible from debts incurred prior to his departure.

Taxation Implication on Leaving

1. Capital Gains Tax

When a partner leaves the partnership he will be treated for capital gains tax purposes as disposing of his fractional share in each partnership asset. However no capital gains tax will actually arise unless either:

(a) he receives actual consideration for such a disposal outside the accounts of the partnership (e.g. a payment for goodwill which has not been valued in the accounts); *or*

(b) the asset has been revalued in the accounts; *or*

(c) the arrangement is of a non-commercial nature.

The capitalised value of a pension or annuity to be paid to an outgoing partner or his dependants will *prima facie* be treated as consideration for the disposal of his assets (s 37(3) TCGA 1992) and hence a charge to capital gains tax will arise. However, SP D12 provides that it will only be so treated if it is more than can be regarded as reasonable recognition for his past contribution of work and effort to the partnership. The SP sets out a table of average shares of profits which the Revenue will consider reasonable for the number of years spent in the partnership. The end result is that very few annuities will in fact give rise to a charge.

2. Income Tax

The closing year rules, see p105 ante, will apply in determining the leaving partner's income tax liability. The remaining partners (if any) will however continue to be taxed on the current year basis.

APPENDIX

Further Reading

British Company Law and Practice, looseleaf, CCH
Farrar, *Company Law* (3rd ed, 1991) Butterworths
Goo, *Minority Shareholders' Protection* (1994) Cavendish Publishing
Gower, *Principles of Modern Company Law* (5th ed, 1995) Sweet & Maxwell
Lindley and Banks, *Law of Partnership* (17th ed, 1995) Sweet & Maxwell
Morse, *Partnership Law* (3rd ed, 1995) Blackstone Press
Pennington, *Company Law* (7th ed, 1995) Butterworths
Pennington, *Corporate Insolvency Law* (1991) Butterworths
Sealy and Milman, *Annotated Guide to the Insolvency Legislation* (4th ed, 1994) CCH
Tolley's *Company Law,* looseleaf, Tolley

Index